Unfamiliar Spirits

Unfamiliar Spirits
Ghosts of the British Isles

KEITH B. POOLE

ROBERT HALE · LONDON

© *Keith B. Poole 1989*
First published in Great Britain 1989

Robert Hale Limited
Clerkenwell House
Clerkenwell Green
London EC1R 0HT

British Library Cataloguing in Publication Data

Poole, Keith B. (Keith Baddeley) 1905–
  Unfamiliar spirits : ghosts of the British Isles.
  1. Great Britain. Ghosts
  I. Title
  133.1'0941

ISBN 0–7090–3825–9

Photoset in Palatino by
Derek Doyle & Associates, Mold, Clwyd.
Printed in Great Britain by
St Edmundsbury Press Ltd, Bury St Edmunds, Suffolk.
Bound by WBC Bookbinders Limited.

Contents

For
Madeline

Illustrations

Between pages 128 and 129

Acknowledgements

Cambridge Collection, Cambridgeshire Libraries: 9. Bolton Museums and Art Gallery: 8. Local studies department, Shropshire Libraries: 10. Priaulx Library, Guernsey: 12. The Société Jersiaise: 11.

All other illustrations by Madeline Poole.

I am also indebted to the owners of houses and colleges for granting permission to photograph their properties.

Acknowledgements

I am most grateful to all the many county and island libraries and librarians, not only for invaluable authentic and documented material, but for much personal guidance and help; to the Society for Psychical Research for the same reason.

I must also thank Mr Peter Bamford, Chester Reference Librarian, for a great deal of help and encouragement throughout the months of research on this book; also Mr David Ashley, Chief Planning Officer of Stroud District Council; Mr Richard Hayward, Trustee of Chambercombe Manor; and Mr J. V. Paul.

Last, but not least, my wife, for without her patience, continual assistance and hard work my book could not have been written.

Introduction

The Oxford Dictionary's definition of the word 'ghost' is: 'An incorporated being. The soul of a deceased person, spoken of as inhabiting the unseen world, or as appearing to the living.' The same dictionary defines 'vision' as 'A revelation supernaturally presented to the mind.' If millions of people all over the world believe in visions of saints, as they certainly do, they must surely believe in ghosts, as millions also do. Whilst respecting the opinions and rights of disbelievers, do they not refute the evidence and testimony of those who believe in and have witnessed such supernatural apparitions, especially when given by highly intelligent people and investigated by the learned Society for Psychical Research?

If it is disputable that disbelievers outnumber believers, the fact remains that publishers have an enormous market for readers in the occult. Librarians assert that series of books on ghosts form one of the most popular to readers, especially when autumn comes, lasting throughout winter until the spring. The greatest mystery is that such books should be read at all in an age of nuclear power, space travel, pilotless planes and ships, journeys to the planets and below the oceans, and walking on the moon – not least, since the invention of electricity by which to read ghost stories, instead of candles, which once created their own atmosphere of apprehension and even fear.

The division between the worlds of paganism and Christianity became the most important factor in the history of the occult. The pagans believed in the finality of death to such an extent that they buried their dead with all they would need to enter the other world: food, drink, tools, clothing and weapons. They neither believed their dead would return nor even wanted them to. Christianity brought belief in the everlasting life and the existence of the soul. There are many examples of earth-bound spirits in ghost history, those whose body has died but whose soul seeks peace and rest in order to enter the other world. More numerous are those who return to earth from the other world.

These are again divided between the evil and the good. The most evil of all are the poltergeists. They are malevolent, especially towards children; such is their power that they finally drive people out of their houses. The good ones are the quiet ghosts, the gentle, caring, benevolent ghosts who return to the castles, abbeys, mansions and cottages where they were happy before death. They have, in some cases, been accepted as a pleasant guest in the house, such as 'Silky' in the story of Denton Hall, or Madame Gould in the Devon story of Lew Trenchard.

As one who has seen two ghosts and felt the enormous power of an unseen one in Berry Pomeroy Castle, Devon (a story in my previous book, *Britain's Haunted Heritage*), I have never for one moment doubted their existence, so I have tried to bring as many as I can into a single book – for one important reason. Every country, county and island of the British Isles has its own special traditions, legends, folklore and ghosts, familiar to all who were born or live there. Thus it is that all those parts of one single heritage are not known to another region. What has emerged is of immense importance, for many of the stories, though they vary considerably from the kernel existent in all of them, are to be found not only in the British Isles but in the whole world of legends, traditions, folk-songs, folklore and ghost stories.

I have, therefore, selected from the masses of material covering ghost history all the little-known or unknown stories, omitting the more famous and oft-repeated ones. The task has been one long joy and discovery which I can only hope will be shared by readers.

1 East Anglia

Cambridgeshire: The Abbey House: The House of Terror

For more than a century the hauntings of the Abbey House in Barnwell, on the outskirts of Cambridge, were so terrible that at one time it was considered to be the most haunted house in England. It stands close to the site of the former Barnwell Priory, a twelfth-century Augustinian foundation. The building is haunted by a large-sized hare known as 'Wolfie', a mysterious nun who stares at sleepers until they wake, the eccentric giant Squire Butler, the disembodied head, a 'furry' dog like a squirrel and finally poltergeists which have presented formidable challenges to its owners, many of whom have fled in terror from the ghost house.

The present house was built in 1678 by Neville Alexander Butler, who in 1714 was succeeded by his grandson Jacob, a bull-headed giant standing six feet four inches, quarrelsome, generous, wealthy, a brilliant barrister, a great eccentric, known as 'the Squire'. His ghost, known as 'the Giant Squire', haunted Abbey House, children always crossing over to the other side of the road to avoid going near it.

Months before his death, Squire Butler ordered a coffin, to be made from a large oak tree on his estate and of such dimensions that several people could have been buried in it. It became a sensation of Cambridge, and anyone wishing to see it was free to do so, at the same time drinking copiously of the wine provided by Butler himself, with pride and joy. One of the legatees in his Will was required to drive the waggon on which was the enormous coffin to Barnwell church. It was to be drawn by Butler's two favourite horses, Brag and Dragon. If his burial there was refused, his body was to be driven back to his own house and buried in a huge grass plot prepared in the garden.

He might have lived much longer had not his beloved dog died. When news of this was brought to him, he said, 'I shall not live long now my dog is dead.' He died very shortly after and lies buried in Barnwell churchyard, where, at the western end, are no fewer than six stone slabs to commemorate him and his ancestors, and with his own autobiographical details. There is no evidence of violence in his ghost, which is just a lonely, wandering but disturbing ghost hunting round the house for his dog. There is also the ghost of a 'furry' dog which is seen wandering about, believed to be the giant Squire's dog looking for its master.

The terrifying ghost of a disembodied head which has driven owners out of the house was described by one owner as recently as fifty years ago as that of a woman with a 'death-white' face suddenly appearing at the foot of a bed, staring down at the sleeper.

The most dependable record of happenings was compiled by Professor F.J.M. Stratton of Gonville and Caius College, Cambridge; after his death in 1961, his file was passed to the Society for Psychical Research, to whom the author of this book is indebted for constant courtesy, valuable help and material of their investigations into the supernatural world. This distinguished professor, who was a colonel in the Royal Engineers, decorated with the DSO and the Legion of Honour, President of Caius College, Fellow of the Royal Society and Lieutenant of the County of Cambridgeshire, was deeply interested in ghosts. He was a serious, level-headed man and actually rented Abbey House for one month to prove the existence of ghosts.

The earliest date mentioned in his detailed account of an owner of the house was early this century, when it was occupied by Mr J.C. Lawson, Fellow of Pembroke College, a most distinguished classical scholar, College and University lecturer in Greek, who served with Naval Intelligence in World War I. The family (Mr and Mrs

Lawson then had two children, two more being born later) moved into Abbey House in October 1903, occupying part of it.

The haunting began on the very first night with an alarming incident. A tremendous bang came on the nurse's door, being repeated on the door of the maids' room. They were all terrified and were unable to console the children, who awoke 'howling disconsolately'. The servants were unwilling to stay but Mrs Lawson persuaded them to change their minds, saying it was their great Newfoundland dog that had made all the noise, trying to go in with the children. However, there were no marks of claws on the freshly painted door.

The next phenomenon was 'the Animal', described in Mr Lawson's own account as '...a nondescript kind of animal resembling a large-sized hare with close-cropped ears. It was always seen and heard running about on its hind legs, the patter of its footsteps being very distinct and characteristic.' Mrs Lawson notes the first appearance of it to her son John in the spring or autumn of 1904. He, however, could not recollect such an animal. His mother said that he, at the age of three, had asked her 'what the little brown thing was'; his father also saw it, some time later. John's little sister also saw 'a lot of little brown things' walking in at the door after her mother had put her to bed, asking her if they were 'wolfies' [wolves].

The most remarkable account of 'Wolfie', as 'the Animal' was now called, was given by Mr Lawson himself: 'It was never seen standing still or moving slowly. Its haunts were the downstairs rooms, – drawing-room and dining-room – the stairs, the upstairs passage and the central parts of the house ... [he] heard it coming along the passage and turning after it passed him got it between himself and the light at the end of the passage. He convinced himself of its hairy outline and of its apparent solidity ....'

The next apparition was 'the Nun', a mysterious figure dressed in black, who always appeared between midnight and four o'clock in the same room. If the times of her appearance were irregular, her habits were the opposite. She would suddenly and noiselessly enter the bedroom

through a locked door that always creaked when opened
by anyone else, move slowly across the room, halt at the
foot of the bed, stare hard at the sleeper until he or she
would be awakened, then glide away and disappear into
the curtains. The Lawson children were afraid of her and
would not sleep in that bedroom. The parents saw her
repeatedly and were never afraid of her. Indeed, Mrs
Lawson grew so annoyed with her that she awakened one
night to make a sign of the cross and say to 'the Nun', 'In
the Name of the Holy Trinity, poor soul, rest in peace.' It
went away through the curtain and was never seen or
heard by her again.

Professor Stratton, in his account of the phenomena of
Abbey House, stated the following for the reason of 'the
Nun's' appearances: 'Local legend connects the phantom
nun of Abbey House with a bricked-up opening still to be
seen in the cellars. This is supposed to mark the end of a
tunnel which allegedly once ran from Barnwell Priory to
the nunnery which occupied the site of Jesus College ...
Mr A.D. Cornell describes how ... he examined the deep
excavations ... Mr Cornell writes: "There was no evidence
of any disturbed ground below a depth of four feet from
the existing ground level anywhere along the entire length
of the cutting." '

This examination was carried out as recently as 1969.
Professor Stratton did not think it impossible that a tunnel
ran either to the river or to Barnwell Priory, both of which
are to the north of Abbey House.

Mr Lawson's ending of his personal account of 'the
Nun' is emphatic that they knew nothing at all of such an
apparition when they first took the house and that it was
he and his wife who had actually christened her 'the Nun';
only when they later found out that the neighbourhood
was reputedly haunted by a nun were they convinced that
what they had seen was no hallucination.

The next disturbances for the Lawsons were not visible
but audible. These were heavy footsteps going up and
down the stairs at night and sometimes in one or other of
the rooms where someone was sleeping. More often than
not, footsteps heavily treading round the room were heard
by the person sleeping below and not by the person

actually in the room. One night the nurse had awakened her mistress to ask who was tramping about in the top attic, which was empty and locked, though her mistress had heard nothing. There was also the apparition of a man in armour sitting in the dining-room, seen by Mrs Lawson.

In a letter dated 22 January 1972, John Lawson wrote a most truthful and authentic account of his parents during their tenancy of Abbey House:

> My parents were staid Edwardians with a staid Victorian up-bringing. I feel quite sure that neither was over-imaginative or predisposed towards belief in the supernatural. I am sure that prior to their own experiences they would have considered such events to have no place outside fiction or folklore. My father had considerable critical ability and would not have accepted his own experiences and recorded them without having carefully tested and cross-examined himself. My mother was a religious woman who would not have accepted them without considerable self-examination.

The Journal of the Society for Psychical Research for September 1972 contains corroboration of the Lawsons' accounts of happenings during their tenancy, if indeed any were needed, in a report on the phenomena in Abbey House since their departure.

Between the years 1911 and 1961 Abbey House continued to be haunted. In August 1920 the south end was occupied by G. Granville Sharp, President of the Union, his wife and his little daughter Charmian. He found his daughter crying bitterly because she had seen 'the Animal', asking if it would hurt her. When assured that 'Wolfie' would not, she was no longer alarmed when she saw it again. In 1940 it was seen by another child. Charmian also saw 'the Nun' 'leaning over her bed and looking at her'.

A health visitor occupied No.1 Abbey House from 1952 to 1955. Arriving in December and being tired, she went early to bed. She recorded being pressed down by what might have been a heavy metal tray; her impression was that it was being held down by the figure of a man 'who seemed to be standing on a higher level'. She managed to switch on the light, but the tray and the man had disappeared. It is the only story that does not agree with the others.

Professor Stratton himself occupied No.1 for a week in 1955 and recorded that persons staying in the house the first time were particularly likely to experience phenomena, but, in spite of most detailed investigation by himself and undergraduates interested in the supernatural, there was no evidence of any hauntings during his stay. Perhaps at last all the ghosts have found peace and quiet, but there are many people in Cambridge, and even beyond, who still wonder.

Cambridgeshire: Corpus Christi College: The College Hauntings

Since 1632 the fourteenth-century Corpus Christi College of Cambridge University has been haunted, and a ghost was certainly seen within the past fifty years.

The apparition of a ghostly figure made continuous visits to its old rooms particularly and to the college generally, so becoming a legend, mostly disbelieved by undergraduates, until in the year 1903 news of disturbances of an alarming nature began to circulate. Two years later the fear had spread throughout the college that there really was something supernatural. As a result of these rumours, in March 1905 *The Occult Review* published an account of the psychical experiences of some of the undergraduates. *The Occult Review* emphasized, however, that, '…they had no experience in psychical research but merely wished to get rid of an unexplained visitor.' The account makes absorbing reading.

At that time the hauntings first reported took place on the left side of the college Old Court, looking onto the New Court, where there were two sets of rooms, one above the other. At one time they served as the Master's

Lodge. The earliest reported sighting was of a head without a body, which sent a terrified undergraduate rushing out into the courtyard. The second sighting was by a Fellow, who was so petrified that he crawled breathlessly on his hands and knees out of the haunted room. Dons and undergraduates alike sneered at the reports. Then in the October term of 1903 unaccountable noises and rappings disturbed sleepers, as well as the violent shaking of the washstand at the foot of the bed of one of the occupants. A year later an undergraduate occupying one of the haunted rooms was suddenly mystified by feeling much unease when he entered his room at three o'clock in the afternoon to do some work; unable to concentrate, he suddenly stood up and looked across the court to a set of rooms opposite where he saw the head and shoulders of a man leaning out of the window. It was a stranger whom he could not recognize; he had long hair and seemed to be glaring at him. The undergraduate watched the man for three minutes, then, suddenly terrified, went downstairs and crossed the court to see who it was, only to find the room door locked. He discovered that it was quite impossible for him to have seen anyone, since the owner had left his room at two o'clock and did not return till 6.30.

Hillier, the occupant of the lower set of the haunted rooms, woke up at five o'clock one morning to find a white figure standing by his bed. It stood motionless for some minutes, then moved across towards the sitting-room and disappeared through the shut door. Hillier was so alarmed that he got up, dressed and left his rooms. Before that, he had been disturbed by loud and inexplicable noises. He told another undergraduate about his experiences and was offered the sitting-room of his set if he wished, but he refused. That same night, however, as Hillier went to his bedroom, he saw the figure of a man standing by the fireplace. In a flash Hillier fled back to his friend and, after telling him what he had seen, accepted the offer to sleep in the sitting-room. The next morning he went to the authorities and refused to occupy the rooms any more.

The noises, however, went on in the rooms above, and

the occupant decided that exorcism was the only solution. A friend in another college who was interested in spiritualism decided he would like to join in the ceremony and would bring four other men with him.

It was a clumsy and amateurish ceremony, begun by all kneeling down, reciting the Lord's Prayer and calling upon the Trinity to command the spirit to appear. Two of the group said they had seen the ghost in a mist that developed into the form of a man, which seemed to be shrouded in white with a gash in its neck, moving slowly about the room; as the two men, holding a crucifix, approached the apparition, they seemed to be forced back by some invisible agent. 'The two men completely broke down, becoming quite unnerved.' The *Occult Review* goes on:

> A few days later they tried again to exorcise the spirit, with exactly the same result: the same men saw it, and no one else. They were again driven back, although this time they approached holding hands. The others allege that they appeared to grow stiff, and that they gripped one another convulsively. The meeting was again broken up without anything definite having been effected.
>
> In this case the *planchette* has been tried with considerable success. The writing is clear and rapid, and some of the communications are as follows 'I'll ruin you'; 'I'll send you mad'; 'I'll ruin every one of you'; and other more forcible and quite unprintable expressions. When asked who it was, and why it was there, it answered through the *planchette*: 'My name is Thomas Hardinge. I killed myself in these rooms in 1707.' They then asked where it lived, and it replied: 'In the fourth panel from the door in the lower room.' ... of Thomas Hardinge nothing has as yet been found. The panel alluded to by the *planchette* was pulled down, but it was discovered to conceal nothing but a bricked-up wall.

If none of the incidents in the *Occult Review* is acceptable to anyone dubious, even distrustful, about the supernatural, there is one ghost in the College who is accepted and has been for centuries. It is the ghost of Dr Butts, Master of the College from 1626 to 1632 and Vice-Chancellor during the outbreak of a disastrous plague in 1630. (It is interesting to know that it was through the dreaded Black Death that Corpus Christi College was founded in 1352, because so many of the clergy had died; fees for Masses for the dead were so high that the Guilds founded the college for the education of clergy who should be compelled to celebrate Masses for the departed members of the Guild.)

The effect of the 1630 plague on Dr Butts was terrible, as he wrote in a letter to the High Steward of Cambridge, describing the pain and suffering of the people, the deaths and the interminable services for the dead: '...myself am alone, a destitute and forsaken man, not a Scholler with me in the College, not a Scholler seen by me without'. He was reported by a contemporary to have become a changed man, roaming about the college and his rooms, having a 'ghost-like' look about him. The last words are prophetic, for on Easter Sunday 1632, as Vice-Chancellor, he was due to preach at the university but never fulfilled the engagement, for he committed suicide in his own room, hanging himself by his garters.

Ever since that time his rooms are said to have been haunted, and it was his ghost that had been seen by the undergraduate at three o'clock that afternoon when, uneased by something, he had seen the head and shoulders of a man leaning from the window of the set of rooms opposite. That was in 1904, almost 300 years later.

The rooms are no longer occupied by undergraduates, but within the last fifty years reports have been made that the ghost of Dr Butts has been seen roaming around the college.

2   The Heart of England

Gloucestershire:Stroud: The Haunted Park

It would be difficult to find a place in this county more reputedly haunted than Woodchester Park mansion. This splendid Cotswold-stone Tudor-style building enclosing a courtyard, with its fifty rooms, bell-tower, fourteenth-century-style vaulted chapel, balcony, stables and gargoyles, stands alone and abandoned in a deep valley, surrounded by a thousand acres of parkland, impenetrable woodland and five lakes, visible only from the air. Every window has been smashed; its chapel and interior have been vandalized; boarded-up parts of the building bear the word 'Danger' in large letters to deter people foolish enough to enter. There is no public access; appointed guides have entry only through the massive five-barred gates with computerized padlocks. The only living things there are the birds and animals (badgers have been filmed in the television series *Badger Watch*), together with the protected colony of horseshoe bats which have taken over one of the rear rooms. According to the planning officer of Stroud District Council, which has recently paid £10,000 towards the cost of the mansion, the bats would be jeopardized by public interference.

In the silence and peace of the whole area, it is difficult to agree with local people and legend that the house is spooky, frightening, eerie and better to avoid. Secret and mysterious as it certainly is, it seems sad and melancholy in its loneliness, and nothing would be easier than to come upon a ghost, even in broad daylight. Indeed, one of them has often been seen: the apparition of a Roman centurion. This is in no way surprising, since Gloucestershire was a favoured place of the Roman legions in the fourth and fifth centuries, during their occupation of Britain. The imposing temples, the rich and splendid villas became empty and abandoned when the fall of Rome began and the legions were hurriedly withdrawn from Britain.

The most palatial of these villas was at Woodchester, excavated by Lysons nearly 1,300 years later, in the eighteenth century. It had over sixty rooms surrounded by baths, gardens and courtyards. The great mosaic, much of which is now in the British Museum, consisted of over a million tiny fragments within a forty-eight-foot square, depicting animals, flowers, birds and leaves, centred by Orpheus playing his lute. One of the smaller villas might well have belonged to the Roman centurion whose ghost haunts the area. He may have been a deserter, unwilling to leave his home to return to his native land, content to stay on because he was happy. The people who have seen him spoke also of a ragged dwarf, not accounted for unless he was a slave. During the occupation the poverty-stricken village of Barnwood was forced to provide slaves for the Romans who possessed rich villas. More than one hundred and fifty graves were excavated long after the Roman legions had departed.

There were other ghosts, however, of a much later period, brought about by all the changes preceding the building of Woodchester Park mansion.

In 1846 William Leigh, a Lancashire man who became a deeply religious Roman Catholic, bought the thousand-acre estate, then called Spring Park, from the second Earl of Ducie, whose ancestor had built a great mansion during the reign of George I. It was on the same site as the present one, commanding a view eastwards, including the five lakes. The only buildings of his day to remain are the tower-like lodge, the ruined stables and the two pairs of entrance gates, one at either end of the valley.

Leigh had been cold-shouldered by his friends because of his religious fervour and beliefs, so he decided to make a new start in another part of the country, choosing Gloucestershire. He at once employed the celebrated architect Pugin to repair and alter the mansion. Pugin, however, had found some letters of Lord Ducie's pointing out the impracticability of repairing the mansion, which was his reason for selling it, and informed Leigh that he was of the same opinion. Such was Leigh's religious zeal and so determined was he to promote Roman Catholicism in a new county that he invited the Superior of the Passionists in Rome to found an establishment at Woodchester. This order, founded by Paolo della Croce in 1720, is described in *The Oxford English Dictionary* as '...the Congregation of Discalced Clerks of the most Holy Cross and Passion of Our Lord Jesus Christ'. 'Discalced clerks' means 'barefooted' monks or nuns of the order.

The Superior, the Venerable Dominic Barberi, arrived on 24 March 1846. It was then that Leigh suggested to Pugin that the Superior should have a monastery and to defer the building of the house, to which Pugin agreed. Unfortunately Leigh quarrelled with Pugin over the siting of the monastery, engaging another architect, Charles Hansom, followed by yet another, Benjamin Bucknall, a local man. The work on the monastery was not completed until 1853, when Leigh's thoughts returned to the house. One of the many mysteries surrounding the monastery is why it was demolished. All that remains of what must have been a fine building, according to Charles Hansom's model in the Arlington Hill Museum at Bibury, are the clear traces of it round the Roman Catholic church beside the A46, on the road to Stroud from Nailsworth.

There have been reported sightings by locals of a ghost of a monk wandering about the grounds of the mansion, which might even have been that of Dominic Barberi himself, or one of a number of monks he probably brought from Rome. It may have been the phantom of a monk who committed suicide in one of the five lakes. An apparition of a black dog is supposed to have brought warning of impending death to any monk.

Work having begun on the new mansion, Leigh moved into 'The Cottage' to the south, still standing – indeed, occupied until quite recently. Leigh never saw the completion of his house, for he died in 1873; it was never really lived in, and work on it was suspended. One of the rooms still has the stonemason's ladder pointing to wooden frames in place as roof supports, almost as if the order to stop had been dramatically given.

It was some time later that other ghosts were reported in

the grounds, both of them more than suspect. One was of a keeper who had been torn to death by guard dogs, probably those used by Leigh to protect the property. The other was of a headless rider on a horse, supposed to have been a suitor of Mrs Leigh. As nothing is known of Leigh's domestic life, this cannot be verified; it would seem to be local gossip.

More authentic ghosts, however, were two American soldiers identified by their uniforms after World War II. These add even more to the mysteries of Woodchester Park mansion. There has been increasing talk that the mansion was used for 'most secret' work carried out in a scientific laboratory in one of the rooms during the war. Whether or not this is true, there is very certainly a most inexplicable room containing a quantity of X-ray material that has never been removed from the house, as no owner has ever come forward to claim it. It is almost impossible to believe that anything of this nature could have been undertaken there, when one sees the mansion as it is today. Nevertheless, 'sightings' of American soldiers have been often reported.

According to the *Victoria County History of Gloucestershire*, the trustees of the Barnwood House Hospital bought 300 acres of land in 1940 which they sold in 1955, but in no sense could the mansion have been used as a hospital.

One day, perhaps, this truly remarkable stone mansion (even the gutters, drainpipes and gargoyles are of stone) will be completed, sold, furnished and occupied by a multi-millionaire, but until then it stands abandoned and alone in a secret silence, with its mysteries and its ghosts. Those who have seen it will surely never forget it as an extraordinary experience, unlikely to be repeated.

Northamptonshire: Althorp: The Ghostly Stableman

Althorp, the magnificent home of Earl Spencer, father of the Princess of Wales, is six miles north-west of

Northampton. It is a treasure-house of pictures, porcelain and fine furniture and, whilst it is open to the public, it is still a private family home. In contrast with the main building is the stable block, built in 1712. It is a grand rectangle of dark ironstone and is the first part of the whole building to be seen by visitors. That a residence of such antiquity and importance should have a ghost is therefore not surprising, though it is of a quiet and faithful groom who, though disturbing, is not at all harmful.

In the early 1800s Mr (afterwards Archdeacon) Drury was invited by the Earl's daughter Sarah, who in 1813 had married the third Baron Lyttelton, to join them in a visit to her father. During their stay they decided to play billiards, and Mr Drury and Lord Lyttelton went up to the billiard room for a game while the others went to bed. The two players found the game so enjoyable that it continued longer than they realized, only stopping when a servant entered the room to request permission to retire, as it was quite late. They apologized to the servant and agreed that they should all go to bed.

Lord Lyttelton said he would extinguish the lights, at which point the servant warned them to be very careful, both in the billiard room and in their own bedrooms, as Earl Spencer had a terrible fear of fire, which would be very dangerous, even fatal, if it spread through such an enormous house. They promised to be careful. When they finished the last game, they were amazed to find that it was after two o'clock when they went to their bedrooms.

Mr Drury had no idea how long he had slept before being awakened by a light shining directly into his face, almost blinding him. He started up in terror that the house was on fire, remembering the warning of the servant, but both the candle and the fire in his bedroom were out. In the light his astonished eyes saw a figure standing at the foot of his bed. He was dressed in a striped shirt and a flat cap, like a stableman, and carried a lantern with the bull's-eye turned full up.

'What do you want, my man? Is the house on fire?' exclaimed Mr Drury. But the man remained silent and immobile, not lowering the lantern a fraction.

'What do you mean by coming into a gentleman's room

in the middle of the night? What business have you here?'
he demanded as he raised his arm to keep the light away
from his face. Still the figure remained silent and motionless. Mr Drury was now very angry and shouted at the
intruder, telling him he was an impudent scoundrel and to
get out of the room. He would report him to his master in
the morning.

The figure very slowly and deliberately lowered the
lantern and passed into the dressing-room adjoining the
bedroom, though there was no exit other than that by
which he had entered from the passage. Mr Drury then
made up his mind not to bother any more about the figure;
it must look after itself. As long as there was no risk of fire,
he saw no point in upsetting himself, so, turning over, he
went to sleep again.

In the morning, when he went down to breakfast, Lady
Lyttelton was already at the table. He told her that he
thought it was a very odd thing that a stableman with a
lighted lantern had come into his bedroom during the
night. He had been very silent and had stood at the end of
the bed. 'I suppose he must have been drunk, though he
did not look so!' He then told Lady Lyttelton how the man
was dressed, at which she turned very pale and looked
frightened.

'You have described my father's favourite groom,' she
said. 'It was always his last duty to go round the house and
see that all the lights were extinguished and everyone safe.
He had strict orders to enter any room if he was suspicious
there was any light.' She paused. 'He died a fortnight ago.'

Northamptonshire: *Ringstead: The Haunted Village*

More than a century has passed since a pretty
nineteen-year-old girl disappeared from the
Northamptonshire village of Ringstead, near Thrapston,

on the A605 road. The mystery of her departure remains unsolved to this day.

On the evening of 22 July 1850 a labourer named Joseph Groom was taking a stroll along a lane past an orchard when he heard angry voices having an argument. He at once stopped to listen, recognizing both the voices. One was that of a girl who was almost hysterical as she shouted: 'I did not intend to meet you here tonight in the orchard for I've got the feeling you intend to kill me. Isn't it so? But it's yours. Yours, I tell you and no one else's.' A man's voice mumbled something angrily that Groom could not hear. Then the girl's voice rose again: 'The Lord have mercy on me if I am to die in my state of sin.' Then there was a long silence, and Groom moved away. Had he entered the orchard instead, the murder of Lydia Atley might never have happened.

The man's voice was that of a prosperous local butcher named William Weekley Ball, who had evidently seduced Lydia, a simple, somewhat 'giddy' girl according to the villagers, who had caused much gossip by her intimate association with a married man. They had been seen too much together, and the village wondered why Ball's wife did nothing about it. Keen watching eyes were not slow in noting Lydia's pregnancy, confirmed next day by Groom's report of the scene in the orchard and the fact that Lydia vanished that very night and might well have been murdered by her seducer. Suspicions erupted into action, and the police were informed.

A not very convincing search was made of the orchard, Ball strongly denied all accusations, and since nothing against him could be proved, the matter was dropped, though never forgotten. His business was boycotted, and he and his wife removed themselves to Ramsey in Huntingdonshire, where he once more created a flourishing butcher's shop.

Fourteen years later, in the winter of 1864, sensation was caused not only in the village but in the whole county when even the London newspapers announced that a human skeleton had been found in a ditch in Keystone Lane, which a group of labourers had been employed to clean out. The police were informed and a doctor was summoned, who decided that the body was that of a young girl between sixteen and twenty years of age. More important still was an aperture in the lower jaw made by a tooth that had been extracted. A man named Dix stated that he had extracted a tooth from Lydia's jaw a fortnight before she disappeared. Once again the evidence of murder seemed conclusive, and Weekley Ball was at once arrested and charged with the murder of Lydia Atley before a magistrate, who committed him for trial on 25 February 1864 at the March Assizes in Northampton.

The evidence, if circumstantial and undoubtedly strong, was defeated by a clever defence counsel. A packed court, quite convinced of Weekley Ball's guilt, even if proved wrong, heard defence tell the judge that before 'Enclosure' of local commons, gypsies had had their caravans sited on land part of which was an unhallowed cemetery used by them for their dead. On 7 March two more skeletons were discovered, and defence counsel urged Mr Justice Crompton to withdraw the charge of murder against Weekley Ball as there was no absolute proof of his guilt. Judge Crompton concurred and the case was dismissed, the accused being released. Ball, whose business in Ringstead had been destroyed, returned to Ramsey as an innocent man. If *he* believed in his innocence, no one else did, and it was then that the hauntings of the village began.

The ghost of Lydia Atley was constantly seen along the lane leading to the orchard, in the orchard, in Meeting Lane, from Cherry Orchard to the church gate, where she always stopped, never entering the church. She wandered about wearily, saddened, clasping her hands and weeping, always finishing up by the place where her supposed body was found. One night in the autumn a village labourer was coming up a lane wheeling a barrow containing some produce from his allotment; just as he got near the Meeting yard, he found he could make no further progress as the barrow wheel was immovable. Lydia Atley was stopping him! He was convinced he had seen her ghost but found that a stick had blocked the wheel. That was the effect the haunting had on the village people.

It was even more serious that nothing altered the total

conviction of the whole village that butcher Weekley Ball had murdered Lydia. All the children were singing a song entitled 'The Cruel Butcher of Ringstead', dancing as they sang through the many verses.

The affair was more seriously taken by the youths of the village of Irthlingborough, who decided to hold their own mock trial by jury. One was chosen to represent Weekley Ball, another for the judge and from the rest the jury. The trial was conducted with mock solemnity. The judge listened to the counsels, summed up and passed sentence on the prisoner, who was led away to the scaffold to be hanged, the others representing the watching public.

Unfortunately one of the mock executions went wrong, when a prisoner was being actually strangled by the rope, something that struck terror into the watchers, so that many of them ran away leaving the boy. He became unconscious and in a few more seconds would have died but was saved just in time. The youths tried to keep quiet about what had happened, but it reached the knowledge of the authorities, and these mock trials were stopped, 'which at that time were common to country districts', as the *Northampton Daily Reporter* recorded on 30 July 1906.

The whole affair could and perhaps should have ended there, but it did no such thing. In the year 1906 the whole case was revived when in late July and early August three local papers, as well as the London papers, reported yet another sensation in Ringstead, forty-two years after the release of Weekley Ball. The papers filled columns announcing the discovery of yet another skeleton of a woman in a field on the Ringstead side of the Thrapston road. Mayes, a farmer's labourer, whilst working, had driven his spade into the skull of a woman, near which were what appeared to be the blade and hasp of a razor. Police and a doctor held an examination of the skeleton, which was pronounced to be that of a woman possibly about thirty years of age.

All the papers gave long accounts of what had happened since the day Lydia Atley disappeared and so revived once more the possibility of yet another inquest. The police and magistrates, however, had no intention of holding another trial, and no inquest took place.

Nevertheless, the case of Lydia Atley and William Weekley Ball has been permanently recorded in every detail and has become an integral part of the legends and myths of Northamptonshire.

Oxfordshire:Oxford University: The Haunted Colleges

In June 1968 a number of the magazine *Isis* headlined one of its articles 'Oxford has the most ghosts', and surely no more convincing proof could be given than the fact that no fewer than nine of its twenty-two colleges have been, and still are, haunted. The two most recent sightings were in 1986 and 1987, already described in my book *Britain's Haunted Heritage*. These are indisputably remarkable stories with authentic documentary evidence of the apparitions seen by students in Magdalen College.

The strangest happening is surely that which occurred in The Queen's College, founded in 1340, an account of which was published in *The Gentleman's Magazine* in 1783. The original record of this was made by the Reverend Mr Mores, formerly of The Queen's College, found in his papers after his death in 1778, which stated the following:

On Sunday, November 18, 1750, Mr Ballard, who was then of Magd. Coll., and myself were talking together at Parker's door. I was then waiting for the sound of the trumpet and suddenly Mr Ballard cried out, 'Lord have mercy upon me, who is that coming out of your college?' I looked and saw, as I supposed, Mr Bonnell, and replied: 'He is a gentleman of our house, and his name is Bonnell; he comes from Stanton Harcourt.' 'My God,' said Mr Ballard, 'I never saw such a face in all my life.' I answered slightly, 'His face is much the same as it always is; I think it is a little more inflamed and swelled than it is sometimes; perhaps he has buckled his band too tight; but I should not have observed it if you had not spoken.' 'Well,' said Mr Ballard again, 'I shall never forget him as long as I live,' and seemed to be much disconcerted and frightened.

This figure I saw without any emotion or suspicion; it came down the quadrangle, came out at the gate and walked up the High Street; we followed it with our eyes till it came to Cat Street, where it was lost. The trumpet then sounded and Mr Ballard and I parted, and I went into the hall and thought no more of Mr Bonnell.

Evening prayers in the college that night were for a seriously ill student, and when Mores asked who it was, he was told it was Mr Bonnell. Mores then said that Bonnell's illness must have been very sudden, for he had actually seen him before dinner that day. The other man said that could not have been possible, for Mr Bonnell had been ill in bed for some days. Confused and puzzled, Mores went away. The next morning Bonnell died. The mystery deepens when one considers that Mores knew Bonnell very slightly and that Ballard, from another college, knew him not at all, yet was frightened, even terrified at what he had seen. Mores' memorandum continued: Bonnell '... was remarkable in his person and his gait and had a particular manner of holding up his gown behind, so that to anyone who had but once seen him he might be known by his back as easily as by his face'.

Merton College, founded 1264, is renowned for its haunted Mob quadrangle, so named because for generations not one ghost but groups of ghosts have gathered there, which in itself causes much speculation as to why they should choose this one of many of the quadrangles in the college. For years a certain room in the college was haunted by its own unknown ghost, but it ceased to be haunted when it became part of the library.

All Souls College, founded 1437, has a strange white-robed ghost in the vicinity of the library, though not part of it as in Merton College. It walks at certain times of the year on the 'dame path' across the Great Quadrangle, from the rear door of the chapel to the library, where it vanishes. It is perhaps one of the souls in the name of the college, but without identity.

Christ Church College, ('The House', as it is called), first named Cardinal College by its founder, Cardinal Wolsey, was established by Henry VIII under its present name in 1546. It has its own royal ghost, since Charles I resided there during the Civil War and has been seen in two forms: one a headless figure wandering about the college grounds after his execution in Whitehall, but more often walking meditatively up and down the cloisters, always dressed in a jet black velvet cloak, which those who saw him considered to be his premonition of death, though not even he could have foreseen the manner of it. Another ghost is that of the garrison commander charged with cowardice by the Royalists for surrendering his troops to the Parliamentarians with suspicious ease. He was taken to one of the college walls in the grounds, blindfolded and shot by a firing-squad for his treachery. His ghost haunts this part as it wanders along a path known as 'Dead Man's Walk'.

Wadham College, founded in 1610 on the site of an old Augustinian priory, has the legendary ghost of a White Monk, who was obviously at one time of that Order. He had been regularly seen walking from the chapel, across the front quadrangle, up the steps into Hall and right up to High Table, where he vanishes. As recently as 28 December 1968 he was seen by the head porter, as a cowled figure in white, standing before the chapel doors and staring at him, before it suddenly vanished. The ghost was seen again in Hall on a late June evening after dinner at High Table, when three 'scouts' were clearing the table. All of them saw the figure, about six feet tall, standing by the old fireplace, though they thought it was a grey figure like a priest or a woman. Other college servants who have been on duty in the office late at night have often heard footsteps outside, always going only one way, but whoever it was has never been seen.

Though Jesus College, founded in 1571, is reputed to have a number of ghosts, they have never been proven. There is one, however, which has been seen not by one undergraduate but by two at the same time and for quite a long while.

An undergraduate named Prys-Jones was talking to another undergraduate at about midnight on a night of full moon in the year 1910. As it was so late and their conversation had ended, they both rose and crossed over to the window, gazing down at the moonlit quadrangle, when to their astonishment they saw a figure pacing up and down. They both recognized it as their tutor, Mr Jenner, and, deciding to play a joke, they followed him. He was pacing the pavement from the dining-hall to the chapel and back again, so, moving quickly downstairs, they slipped into the darkness and followed him noiselessly at a distance of some ten yards. After a little time Prys-Jones began to whistle Jenner's favourite hymn, 'All through the night', and they were astonished that he did not take any notice, nor even turn round to see who was whistling at that time of night. Instead he continued walking, before turning about and coming towards them, so that they both saw his face and the white tie he wore, resembling that worn by a Nonconformist minister. They also about-turned and followed him back towards the College Hall, where he walked straight through a six-foot-thick wall and vanished.

When they had recovered from the shock of what they had seen, they searched through the ivy-covered wall to find a doorway, but there was nothing there. They were now very frightened, to such an extent that Prys-Jones's friend said he was too terrified to go back to his own rooms and slept on a settee in his friend's room. They made very discreet enquiries next day as to the movements of Jenner the night before, only to be told that he was not even in College as he was staying with friends in Wolvercote. To the end of their lives they knew that what they had both seen was positive, clear and very frightening.

New College, founded 1379, has the authentication of its chapel ghost from Dr David Lumsden, Fellow of the College and a most distinguished organist. In 1962 he was clearing up the books and papers left by the students he had sent to Hall after prolonged rehearsals before he went to turn off the lights and leave. He was accustomed to be in dark churches. He had walked about five paces along the aisle when he suddenly halted. There, seated in the Warden's stall was the figure of a man with a very white face. Dr Lumsden's own story was given in *Isis* in June 1968:

> It was not a blur of light but a definite face with all normal features. The body must have been dark because it was not visible in the pitch darkness of the chapel. I assumed it was in academic or priestly dress. It turned away and walked on for a few paces. Then I realised what I had seen and I ran all the way out of the chapel. I was terrified and since that time I have never stayed alone in the chapel after dark.
>
> Some of the college members have tried to persuade me that what I saw was the ghost of Warden Spooner whose description tallied with what I saw. I do not know who it was and I have no rational explanation for it.

Trinity College, founded 1535, has an almost identical story, with this time a female ghost seen in 1959.

At ten o'clock on a summer night the college verger was making his nightly tour of inspection. The clock was striking the hour, and on the last stroke something made him look up. There, standing some ten feet away, was a lady dressed all in black and smiling straight at him from a beautiful face. They both stood for fully a minute, as he recorded, before he moved a few paces forward towards her as she vanished. He was more overcome than afraid but as he calmed down he suddenly realized the face was strangely familiar. In his own words he states: 'When I got back to my house I looked on the mantelpiece at the photograph of my dead mother and I suddenly realized who the figure was.'

He was eighty-four years old when he told this story and had never seen the figure again.

There are at least six other colleges that claim to have ghosts but there is no authentic documentation of any of them, whereas those written about here have all been witnessed, accepted by those who believe in the supernatural and considerably disturbing rational thinkers.

Shropshire:Chetwynd and Edgmond: Madam Pigott

For many years after her death, the whole countryside surrounding Chetwynd Hall in Shropshire was continually haunted by the sad and terrifying apparition of Madam Pigott, as she was called. Had it not been for her constant appearances, seen by all the villagers and always frightening them, the whole story of her activities would have been just a legend, passed from mouth to mouth by the inhabitants of the villages. It was her persistence and visual restlessness towards the end of the eighteenth century that confirmed the belief of all those who saw her that she was a ghost, and a real ghost. The greatest difficulty is to establish which one of the successive Madams Pigott who lived in the old family mansion of Chetwynd Hall was the ghost.

Tradition has it that one of the marriages was very unhappy and that when Madam Pigott was expecting a child the doctor who came to attend was shocked to find the condition she was in, both mentally and physically. He was so concerned that he warned the husband that his choice must be made between his wife and the child, and was horrified to hear the husband's terse, indifferent, cruel reply: 'One should lop the root to save the branch.' In fact, neither mother nor child survived, so that it is no wonder that her spirit could never rest.

Almost at once, night after night, exactly at midnight, her spirit issued from a trap-door in the roof of Chetwynd Hall, where she died, and began wandering in all parts of the grounds surrounding the mansion and out and along the lanes in the direction of Edgmond village. Her ghost would pause on the way to overturn a large boulder-stone by the roadside between Edgmond and Newport.

Her next favourite haunt became a steep, dark,

high-banked lane known locally as Cheney Hill, but from
then on called 'Madam Pigott's Hill'. Near the top of it was a
curiously twisted tree-root where she used to sit, called
'Madam Pigott's Armchair'; this disappeared in 1877 to
form part of a neighbouring house's garden. Another place
she favoured was the stone wall of Chetwynd Park, where
on moonlit nights she could be seen 'combing her baby's
hair'. Her most terrifying action there was to watch (sometimes from a seat on the branch of a tree) for a belated rider
to pass, perhaps in search of a doctor or midwife; she would
then spring up behind him, not with her baby but with her
black cat, clinging hard to the rider's back and not releasing
him or her until they reached a running stream, where she
would vanish.

The villagers became more and more terrified, never
daring to venture out at night. Protests began to be made to
the local priest, the much-loved and respected Mr Foy,
curate of Edgmond, who died in 1816, aged sixty-one,
having been curate for twenty-nine years. During this time
Chetwynd Hall had been put up for sale, doubtless because
of the haunting of Madam Pigott's ghost, for she never left
it.

Mr Foy decided to have the spirit exorcised, not an easy
task in those times, for in Shropshire it required an
assembly of twelve clergymen to carry out the ritual,
though in other counties nine priests were sufficient. Once
they were all assembled, they would settle down to read the
Psalms until they achieved a uniformity of opinion that the
spirit of the deceased was at rest. Mr Foy had the credit of
having been the one to succeed in this, '…for he continued
to "read" after all the others were exhausted'.

This account of Madam Pigott's exorcism, as given by
Charlotte Burne in her *Shropshire Folklore*, 1883, has a
delightful variation in F. H. Groome's *In Gypsy Tents*,
written three years earlier, as told to him by the gypsies:

> … they got twelve priestes, and they were all round a table
> with the bottle on it and candles lighted all round. And
> they all began to pray as hard as they were able, and they
> kept on till it seemed no mannerable good, and they were
> very near giving it up; but the oldest of them told them to

stick to it, and their candles went all out but his, and he prayed till the sweat dropped off his hair. All the rest, you know, were so afeared; and if his candle went out the devil would have fetched them, and she would have scratted them all to pieces ... and as fast as they lighted the candles they were blown out, all but this one; and the priest as belonged to that, he prayed and prayed; and at last they saw her come in between the candles, drawing to the mouth of the bottle, and they kept on praying as hard as ever they could. Long and by last they got her in. And then she begged of them not to be thrown into the Red Seas; but the priest he wouldn't hear of it, and so they threw her in, and the place has been in quietness ever since.

Shropshire:Minsterley: The Haunted Lead Mines

One of the most remarkable ghost stories in Shropshire particularly, and in the United Kingdom generally, is the legend of Wild Edric, who for centuries has haunted the west Shropshire lead mine of Minsterley. There were always people who believed in him, and maybe there are some even today, convinced that he is still alive, though he officially died in the eleventh century. He cannot die, it has always been believed, until all the wrong in the world has been put right and England has returned to the state it was in before the troubles of his day!

The miners called Wild Edric and his band 'the Old Men', and if ever they heard them 'knocking', it was because they had found the best lodes. Only rarely were they permitted to be seen, and that event was dreaded, for it meant that war was about to break out; Wild Edric, at the head of his horsemen, would emerge and move swiftly towards the attack. It was a sure sign the war was going to be serious.

Although Wild Edric has become a legendary figure in the folklore of Shropshire, he was very much a real person and a powerful and influential one during the troubled period following the Norman Conquest of England. He was a nephew of Streona, Ealdorman of Mercia, whose dead body was thrown beyond London Wall by order of Canute, because he had betrayed King Edmund at the Battle of Ashingdon. Wild Edric is mentioned in the Domesday Book as 'Edric Salvage' or 'Silvaticus', possessor of several manors in the days of Edward the Confessor. Very early in the Conqueror's reign, in 1067, Edric was in arms against him, refusing to submit to the new king, in alliance with two of the Welsh kings, who had joined Harold at the Battle of Hastings. The three armies swept into Herefordshire, driving the Normans as far back as the River Lugg, defeating the garrison of Hereford and returning to Shropshire with enormous booty.

Two years later, in the great rebellion of the English in almost every shire. Edric's forces besieged Shrewsbury, then garrisoned by the Normans, but by the year 1070 the risings in the north had been crushed. It was then that Edric 'made peace' with the King; it is nowhere said that he 'submitted'. In fact, only two years later he joined forces with the King against the Scots. This may well have been a clever subterfuge of the King's to keep this border champion under his control, though this is not certain. This is virtually the last authentic record of Edric's life. One chronicle suggested that he died in prison, another that all his estates passed into the hands of the evil Ralph Mortimer of Wigmore.

The mystery of his end is added to by the fact that the haunted lead mines are in that part of Shropshire which contained the estates and manors of Edric during his lifetime, which is the reason why so many people refused to believe he was dead. It was believed he returned to his own territory, together with his wife and knights, to continue his attacks upon any enemy, wherever it threatened.

The legend of Wild Edric seems to have sprung from a young illiterate woman who gave the account of it to her mistress, who in turn repeated it to Charlotte Burne, who related it in her book *Shropshire Folklore*, published in 1883.

This woman, who came from Rorrington, told her mistress that Wild Edric was a bad man, a 'Cong-kerry'. When her mistress asked her what that meant, she replied: 'Why, he used to hang up men by the heels because they were English.' There does not seem to be much sense in the remark, since Edric himself was English and no friend of the Normans who had taken all his lands.

In 1854 Wild Edric and his horsemen were seen and became a warning of what was to come, for the Crimean War was about to break out, a war which was to last two years, described by that great historian G. M. Trevelyan as '...merely an expedition to the Black Sea made for no sufficient reason because the English people were bored by peace'.

Was there perhaps another reason for Wild Edric to lead his horsemen, dressed for battle, out of the mine? According to the documented records of the Shropshire Lead Mines:

> In the 1850s the area experienced a substantial boom in which several new companies were promoted on the London Stock Exchange to work existing mines and sink new ones. The new companies brought to the area Cornish engineers who erected the characteristic Cornish engine houses with their prominent chimneys wherever they were necessary. With no exception the ventures of the 1850s failed, for prices fell yet again and this ruined the companies, most of which had been started with insufficient funds to hand.

This disastrous position for the miners was increased no doubt by the cessation of the 'knockings' which they so implicitly believed to be harbingers of good lodes. It is interesting to note that the Cornish tin-miners themselves also believed in the 'knockings' and actually always left a portion of the food they brought for their lunch to the 'knockers' in order to keep the good lodes going. Such beliefs were far more important for the lead-miners than the possibility of a war. Indeed, this was borne out much later, when Wild Edric and his horsemen made no exit from the mines as a warning for World War I or World War II. Nevertheless, one of the authorities on Shropshire legends states: 'The people say that the miners always do seem to know when a war is going to be desperate.'

The dread which Wild Edric brought to mankind, and the fact that to see him inevitably caused blindness or even madness, is closely linked to the far more renowned legend of the Wild Hunt of mythology found all over northern Europe, originating with Woden on his white horse leading the hunt across the skies, bringing death or disaster to all who watched him pass. Woden, the victory-bringer, the war god, sounding his horn, riding at the head of his Einherjar, the chosen warriors, the spirits of the brave who have fallen in battle, has, in turn, passed into the legends of England among the heroes who have fallen in battle and will return again – King Arthur, King Harold, Hereward the Wake and Thomas the Rhymer.

The coming of them all is supposed to be preceded by the sound of a horn; Wild Edric carried both horn and sword to rouse the dead spirits. This is particularly noticeable in the legends of King Arthur, 'the once and future king'. He lives today in the legends of Cornwall, Somerset, Northumberland, Wales, Scotland and even Switzerland. In Richmond Castle, Yorkshire, King Arthur and his knights are supposed to lie sleeping in the vaults below the ruins, to be roused again by a blast from the horn lying on a table by the entrance, which was discovered by a farmer who, knowing the legend, dared not blow the horn.

The first recorded people to see the legendary Wild Edric were a lead-miner and his daughter at Minsterly mine. They watched in astonishment and fear as he led his troop of armed horsemen out of the mine, in a furious dash towards their target, wherever that was. Every detail of what they saw has been recorded as an unforgettable experience. The father at once shouted to his daughter to cover her face with her hands, or she would go mad. She obeyed him, but she watched the riders through her spread fingers. She described Edric himself as a dark man with curly black hair and flashing black eyes. He was dressed in a short green cloak and coat, with a green cap with a white feather, a horn and a short sword hanging from his golden belt. By his side rode his wife, Lady Godda. She had wavy golden hair loosely hanging to her waist; round her forehead she wore a band of white linen with a golden ornament on it. The rest of her dress was green, and she had a short dagger at her waist. The miner's daughter watched them going out of sight over the hills towards the north.

It was the second time her father had seen them. The former time Wild Edric and his horsemen were going southward: Napoleon Bonaparte in 1806 had issued his Berlin Decree to block the British Isles, being rumoured to have landed on the English shores himself, to study the exact location for a naval invasion.

It is sad that the Shropshire Lead Mines report records that the last remaining mine, Snailbeach, one of the richest in Europe, continued to work only until 1911, 'by which time it was empty of ore'. Since then the lead-mining industry of Shropshire has never recovered. There must be miners living today who still believe in Wild Edric and continue to believe that the 'knockings' have not ceased for the last time. For them the hauntings of the mines will always be felt, and maybe there is a horn hidden somewhere in those derelict mines where Wild Edric and his horsemen wait to be roused.

Warwickshire: Edgehill: The Battle of Ghosts

On the Saturday before Christmas 1642, between twelve and one o'clock in the morning, some shepherds and travellers in the countryside between Warwickshire and Northamptonshire were astonished to find the peace and quiet suddenly shattered by the most unusual noises which, as they drew nearer, became louder; in terror they began to run away. In Lord Nugent's *Memorials of John Hampden* he cites a pamphlet describing what must be the most remarkable account of a ghostly battle in the sky in the history of the supernatural, even more remarkable than those witnessed on Souter Fell and Inveraray.

... on a sudden, whilst they were in their cogitations, appeared in the air the same incorporeal soldiers that made these clamours, and immediately, with ensigns displayed, horses neighing, which also to these men were visible, the alarum or entrance of this game of death was one army which gave the first charge, having the King's colours, and the other the Parliament's at their head, to the front of the battle, and so pell-mell, to it they went. The battle appeared to the King's forces having at first the best, but afterwards to be put to apparent rout. But till two or three in the morning in equal scale continued this dreadful fight, the clattering of arms, noises of cannon, cries of soldiers, so amazing and terrifying the poor men that they could not believe they were mortal or give credit to their eyes and ears; run away they durst not, for fear of being made a prey to these infernal soldiers, and so they, with much fear and affright, stayed to behold the success of the business, which at last suited this effect. After some three hours' fight, that army which carried the King's colours withdrew, or rather, appeared to fly; the other remaining, as it were, masters of the field stayed a good space triumphing and expressing all the signs of joy and conquest, and then, with all their drums, trumpets, ordnance and soldiers, vanished.

After their long and terrifying ordeal, those who had watched such a strange miracle, for it could be nothing else, hurried at once to Kineton in Warwickshire, where they knocked up the magistrate William Wood, who at once called in the local minister, his neighbour Samuel Marshall, who was equally dumbfounded at what they had been told and had the story attested on oath by each of the men who had witnessed the incredible spectre in the sky. Had they not sworn on oath, both magistrate and minister would have dismissed the whole story as imagination or the effects of drink, but the integrity and sincerity of the witnesses were undoubted. Nevertheless, they decided to suspend their judgement until the following night.

On the next night, the original group who had first seen the celestial battle, together with Wood and Marshall and a very considerable number of people from the surrounding parishes, stood in wonder as the battle in the sky was re-enacted; even more so when it was seen again on the following Saturday and Sunday.

There can be no doubt that the most dedicated believer in the supernatural must query the pamphlet's authenticity. The battle of Edgehill was the first battle to be fought between two English armies since Bosworth Field in Leicestershire on 22 August 1485. The Royalist army under Charles I met the Parliamentary army under Essex on 23 October 1642, the first battle of the Civil Wars and recorded historically as a draw. The appearance of the apparitions to the shepherds and travellers was two months later, and, as Lord Nugent points out, when King Charles was informed of the astounding and wonderful story (he was then at Oxford), he at once ordered Colonel Lewis Kirke, Captain Dudley, Captain Wainman and three other officers to attend and enquire into the matter and corroborate the wondrous story, which, as a devout man, the King believed was a portent from God. Lord Nugent continues:

...first hearing the true attestation and relation of Mr Marshall and others, stayed there till the Saturday night following, wherein they heard and saw the forementioned prodigies, and so on Sunday, distinctly knowing divers of the apparitions, or incorporeal substances, by their faces, as that of Sir Edmund Varney, and others that were there slain, of which upon oath they made testimony to His Majesty. What this doth portend God only knoweth, and time perhaps will discover; but doubtlessly it is a sign of His wrath against this land, for these civil wars, which He in His good time finish, and send a sudden peace between His Majesty and Parliament.

To attempt to disqualify this story in any way would be folly indeed, for the documents are authentic enough and the number of witnesses considerable, so perhaps it is best to accept it as a very remarkable supernatural event requiring faith rather than reason.

3   London and the Home Counties

Berkshire:Hurley: A Manifestation of Monks

In 1924 Colonel Rivers-Moore, an archaeologist, bought Ladye Place, a Victorian house erected on the site of a Tudor mansion built by Sir Richard Lovelace 'out of money gotten with Sir Francis Drake'. He did so for a singular and personal reason. This was to bring much disturbance to the peace and quiet of the village of Hurley.

The fact that he was early aware of the mansion's being haunted by a Grey Lady in no way frightened him as it would most people; indeed, it increased his enthusiasm. He had bought the mansion because he was totally convinced that somewhere in or deep below the foundations he would be able to excavate for the coffin containing the body of Editha, sister of Edward the Confessor, who had been buried somewhere in the crypt of Hurley Priory, founded as a Benedictine monastery in 1087. (It must be emphasized that the present Ladye Place is not the original Tudor mansion.) There was abundant evidence of an earlier Saxon foundation to support the Colonel's conviction about the remains of Editha, and as soon as he had made Ladye Place habitable, he began his excavations.

He had personally seen nothing at all of the Grey Lady; what he did see was another apparition altogether. It was the sudden appearance of a monk wearing the Benedictine habit, pointing directly at a part of the wall of the room which indicated a hidden fireplace. Then, as suddenly as the monk had appeared, he vanished. The Colonel was not in any way scared but puzzled, even more so on the following day, when in another room a second monk suddenly appeared, also once more pointing towards the wall and making signs of digging, before vanishing. The Colonel, now excited, at once began digging and opening up the wall. There was a fireplace but, when that was pulled out, another very ancient one was revealed, which the Colonel was now convinced was a part of the priory. He had now formed a small team to help in his excavations, though still keeping his real purpose a secret from them.

The first monk did not return and some weeks passed before a third appeared, also habited like a Benedictine. He was not calm as the others had been but seemed much excited, pointing not to the wall but downwards. He also kept lifting his hands to his head, palms spread and fingers upward, then cupping his hands as if holding something. He, too, then vanished, this time leaving the Colonel confused and wondering what the monk's message meant. It was quite a long time afterwards that he thought out the problem.

However he arrived at some solution is difficult to believe, but legend says he guessed that the name of the monk was King, because the raising of his arms to his head seemed to indicate a crown; either that or the crown meant Henry VIII and the Dissolution of the Monasteries. The monk had perhaps hidden some part of the priory's treasure, as so many did at that time, or perhaps he had stolen something and hidden it. In any case, the team began to dig again, this time downwards at the spot the monk had indicated; after a long time a dried-up well was discovered in which was hidden a casket of medieval jewellery.

By now the Colonel was positive he would discover Editha's coffin, but still the Grey Lady had not appeared. Then, as the casket was hauled to the surface, the Colonel's secret intention had to be revealed, even more so when that same night the monk appeared again, his face smiling and his hands moving in a gesture of blessing and thanksgiving, before vanishing. He was never seen again. The next day, however, one of the team told the Colonel that he 'sensed' a presence, which in some strange way he could not explain and which seemed to be encouraging him to do something he did not understand.

The Colonel himself was now more convinced than ever that he would find Editha's tomb in the end, guided as he was by the helpful monks. All his enquiries and personal research proved that far below Ladye Place was the crypt which had been the burial place of the Benedictine monks, which was part of the old priory. When Henry VIII dissolved the monasteries and religious houses, he was particularly harsh with the Benedictine monks, command-ing that they be dismissed from their priory, which he ordered to be ransacked of all their treasures; it then fell into rack and ruin. It was on part of the site of this priory that the present Ladye Place was built, in sharp contrast to the long refectory adjoining the cloisters, all that remains of the external features of the priory, the rest of it below the long narrow nave of the parish church of St Mary.

There is a splendid heraldic monument to Sir Richard Lovelace and his son Sir Richard in the church. John, a descendant, headed a plot to overthrow the Catholic James II and invite William of Orange to become the Protestant king of England. Macaulay wrote of this plot's being laid 'in the dark chambers below'. John Lovelace afterwards entertained William of Orange in the magni-ficent Elizabethan mansion of Ladye Place his ancestor had built.

John's prodigality and extravagance were so great that he was compelled to sell part of the estate to pay his debts, the title becoming extinct in 1736. It is interesting to note that Kelly's directory for Berks, Bucks and Oxon of 1883 states that in the year 1838 (the year in which Ladye Place was demolished) the bodies of three Benedictine monks in their habits were found in the monastery vault.

The driving motive of the Colonel's excavations was derived from a document of the reign of Richard II which had been buried in the old Benedictine priory, said to contain evidence supporting the Colonel's belief in the location of Editha's tomb and was the reason for the help the monks were giving him to find it. For the next twenty-three years he became more and more obsessed by his convictions, during which time more monks continued to appear, causing such confusion and fear that rumours spread far beyond the village of what was occurring in Ladye Place. Guests and members of the team alike were disturbed by the ghostly appearances.

Out of curiosity to see the legendary Grey Lady, the Colonel's brother-in-law came to stay for a few days, but he went down to breakfast the first morning badly shaken, saying he could not stay another night. He had not seen the Grey Lady but a monk in a black cowl and black habit, who was not at all friendly. He would say no more about it and left at once, never to return to Ladye Place. Another guest later had the same experience and also left. A third guest, a lady, also saw the monk, was very frightened and also did not return. One or two members of the team left. The Colonel himself was becoming increasingly disturbed, since the monks had always been kind to him, and he could not understand why they were frightening his guests, unless it was to keep them away altogether, to allow the Colonel to continue his work, of which the monks evidently approved.

The one monk who most often appeared whenever the Colonel was in a room was the one who walked up and down, his arms folded crosswise on his breast, his eyes closely watching what the Colonel was doing.

At last the Colonel himself thought he ought to do something more than just excavate. He got in touch with a medium to hold a seance to try to find a satisfactory solution to the constant hauntings. The most important thing was to find out from the monks if Editha's tomb really was hidden somewhere, and if so, where. The seance did nothing to clarify the problem.

Some time passed before another seance was organized; this time the team were to attend. The result was dramatic, for one of the ghosts summoned by the medium told them that, if they followed his instructions, they would find the actual foundations of the priory, beyond where they were working in Ladye Place. With much excitement, the Colonel obeyed the instructions, considerably harder work in the surrounding grounds finally revealing a deep, hard base, resembling what might have been a Saxon shrine, under which were buried what were undoubtedly human remains, impossible to identify, but no sign of Editha's coffin or her tomb.

The ghosts continued to appear, but at much longer intervals; the cost of the excavations increased more and more, so that the Colonel at last felt compelled to abandon what was evidently a lost cause, seemingly supported by the cessation of visits by the monks, most especially the absence of the monk who had walked up and down, his arms closely folded.

In 1947 the Colonel finally put Ladye Place up for auction. The house was divided and sold in three lots, which can be seen today in a closed courtyard adjoining the parish church. The Colonel moved first to Wargrave, then to Scotland, dying in 1965.

On a recent visit once more to see Ladye Place, the author was informed by a churchwarden that the lady occupying the cloisters house saw the ghost of a Benedictine monk some twelve years ago. She had not been at all frightened by its appearance, as it seemed quite harmless. After nearly a thousand years since the Benedictine priory was founded, this is indeed remarkable and a challenge even to those who do not believe in ghosts.

Buckinghamshire: Haddenham: The Murder Warning

It was in the evening of Saturday 25 October 1828 that one of the most remarkable experiences in the history of the supernatural took place.

Mrs Edden was in the kitchen of her cottage in Thame, where she was ironing, awaiting her husband's return from Aylesbury Market, where he regularly went on that day, always leaving before dark to do the 1½ hour journey home in his horse and cart. She suddenly looked up to see her husband standing opposite her. For a moment she believed he had come silently into the room to surprise her. Then, petrified with fear, she saw a man she recognized as Benjamin Tyler standing behind her husband. His arm was raised, and clutched in his hand was a heavy stone-hammer which he swung down, striking her husband, who collapsed on the ground. Then the vision vanished as she rushed out screaming into the street to rouse the village, shouting out that her husband had been murdered. Neighbours who had dropped their work ran out and tried to pacify her, but she swore she had seen him murdered and that they must all search for him.

So insistent was she about what she had seen, and which she was now convinced was the truth, that the men went for their lanterns and, accompanied by Mrs Edden, set out along the road they all knew so well. They had walked some distance without seeing any trace of a body, and had already decided they could not go any further, when Mrs Edden, exhausted by the walk and her own emotions, collapsed on the road; the search was abandoned to take her back home, uncertain if what she had said was a delusion or a reality.

Next morning the whole village was roused again by a farmer's labourer. He had taken his horses out early to the grazing-fields of Anxey Meadows near the village of Haddenham, where he found the body of 'Noble' Edden, whose 'head had been bashed in and was a terrible sight', as the man stated at the subsequent trial of the murderers.

The hue and cry was raised, the constable sent for and a band of men set off at once to find the body. The horse and cart were some distance from where the body was found; it was brought to the Cider House in Thame and left there to await the inquest, which was held a few days later, the coroner's verdict being that Edden had been murdered by 'a person or persons unknown'. This convinced no one, least of all the widow, who had seen the murderer commit the crime and knew who he was.

The body was brought back to the cottage, and the widow at once sent word to Benjamin Tyler, demanding that he come at once to prove his innocence or guilt by touching the body of her husband. It was generally believed in those days that a murderer who dared to touch the body would prove his innocence if no sign were given of accusation, whereas if blood flowed from the ears or mouth of the deceased, or the face changed colour, he was guilty. Tyler refused to come.

No one in that room any longer doubted the extraordinary vision Mrs Edden had seen and told them about, for it had been a terrible warning from some unseen power, a premonition of violent death. Soon the suspicion spread across the whole countryside. 'Noble' Edden was buried in the west end of Thame churchyard and a tombstone erected, giving his name, date of death and age, and stating that he was murdered. For many years the countryside round Haddenham was haunted, long after the murderers had been brought to justice.

Mrs Edden's vision was made even stranger by facts of which she had had no knowledge at all during her husband's lifetime.

Edden was called 'Noble' because he was a very handsome young man, extremely strong, a match for anyone in a fight. He was an active, hard-working market gardener, whose small nursery of trees and shrubs was cultivated in Crendon fields on high ground, surrounded by miles of open countryside, so that he could see what was going on in any direction. One day, early in the morning, he saw a suspicious movement in a field not a great distance from where he was standing. He began watching more intently. Two men were walking furtively towards a flock of grazing sheep. Suddenly there was confusion and disturbance as the men bent down and killed one of the sheep as the others fled. As they stood up, he recognized both men from Thame as they dragged the dead sheep away.

At that time sheep-stealing was serious enough to be punishable by transportation for life, or by death. There could be no appeal. He decided to say nothing.

Later that day the farmer, finding one of his sheep missing, informed the constable, and investigations began, but without result.

By his silence 'Noble' Edden became his own worst enemy, for his subsequent stupidity brought about his own death. He told no one for some days, not even his wife; now that he had not informed against them, he was divided between pity for the two men who had committed such a crime and his shame at not informing, solving his problem by letting the culprits know that he knew, without actually telling them. It was then that his stupidity began.

Every time he met them, either in the street or in the bar of an inn, he would bleat at them, crying 'baa, baa, baa', nodding his head with meaning. As the victims were not very intelligent men, they did not at first grasp the meaning of his bleating, but as it was so continuous, it at last dawned on them what he meant and that something would have to be done to silence him.

Weeks, even months, passed and still, in spite of the increasing suspicion, rumours and gossip, no one was arrested. The fact that Edden had not told his wife anything about the sheep-stealers worried him, and he himself began to have fears for his life. This was later borne out by Thomas Bass, who had been given a lift by 'Noble' Edden on the night he had been killed. He lived at Haddenham and was glad to have the lift, but was slightly disturbed when Edden suddenly said he had a feeling that '...something was going to happen to him, something terrible but he didn't know what'. He then said he couldn't tell why he had told him but he felt he must tell someone about his feelings. Bass, alarmed at what Edden said, offered to go on to Thame with him and then walk back across the fields to Haddenham, but Edden said he was all right now he had told his feelings to someone, so Bass got down, though by no means feeling easy about what he had heard.

Though, after the immediate shock of Edden's murder, the affair died down a bit, the people of Thame could not forget it, and it all flared up again about ten months later, in August, when Constable Seymour arrested a man named Sewell on a petty offence, who, under cross-examination, confessed that Tyler had some connection with the murder. A search for him was at once made, for he had left Thame, and he was discovered and arrested. When he was brought before the magistrates, they refused to believe Sewell's charge against him, saying that there was no proof, discharging Tyler. He celebrated his freedom by buying enough ribbons to cover his jacket and adorn his hat, dancing around the town before the houses of all those who had previously given evidence against him, behaving like a madman.

A few days later Sewell was discharged but on leaving prison was immediately re-arrested on a charge of fowl-stealing and sent to Oxford, where he was sentenced to fourteen years transportation. In order to avoid this harsh sentence, he confessed to his part in the murder, hoping to have his sentence altered or reduced, at the same time swearing on oath that Tyler had, in fact, done the actual brutal murder by striking Edden dead with a stone-hammer.

The trial took place on Friday 5 March 1830 and lasted the whole day, for there were a great number of witnesses. Mrs Edden's account of her vision was very lengthy, and she swore a solemn oath that she had seen the murder and the murderer at the very moment it took place. Mr Andrews, the magistrate, listened to the story of her vision patiently but made no comment on it. The only light relief of the day came from Sewell's mother: when the magistrate asked her if she really was the mother of the accused, she answered that she was quite sure but, as she had twenty-four children, it was often difficult to know who was who.

The trial, fully reported in the *Annual Register* 1830 ended with sentences of death being passed on Solomon Sewell and Benjamin Tyler for the wilful murder of William Edden. Outside Aylesbury Gaol a crowd of between four and five thousand people had assembled to see the execution take place, as was customary in those days. An execution usually had to be carried out within forty-eight hours, but the law stated that those sentenced on a Friday must be executed on a Monday, since the Sabbath was a holy day. On Monday 8 March the vast crowds quite early gathered again to watch the scaffold being erected and the murderers brought out. Both men declared they were 'as innocent as babes'.

Sewell behaved quite foolishly, but Tyler was nervous and trembling as he shouted to the crowd that he died an innocent man. The executioner drew the black caps over the heads of both men, and the execution by hanging was quickly carried out.

In *Sketches of the Bucks Countryside*, Mr Harman has preserved for ever the whole amazing story of the apparition that appeared to Mrs Edden at the exact time of the murder. He had been told the story by a very old man whose grandfather had repeated it over and over again and who had actually passed the spot where the murder took place, hearing the quarrel leading up to it. His dog had growled fiercely and his horse had shied and had to be held back but, not wanting to interfere, the grandfather had continued his journey.

For many years the place was shunned by everyone, many people reporting seeing 'Noble's' ghost. His most recent appearance was reported in the *Reader's Digest* at the end of an account of the murder: 'Noble Edden's ghost has been seen in a lane which branches off to Haddenham from the A418; it is said that whoever meets it will suffer bad luck.'

What makes this story unique is Mrs Edden's vision not only of the murder but of the murderer, immortalized in the folklore of Buckinghamshire.

Hertfordshire: *Cheshunt: The Speaking Ghost*

According to Howitt's *History of the Supernatural*, Mr Chapman, the 'well-known London publisher', wishing to live in the country, in about 1830 rented a house on a seven-year lease in Cheshunt, within easy reach of London, from Sir Henry Meux, whose distinguished family lived at Theobalds Park nearby. It was a well-built residence, furnished tastefully, and had a considerable amount of land surrounding it. The family moved in, and Mr Chapman joined them once or twice a week, depending on the amount of work he had in London.

They had been in the house some time, with nothing causing them any disturbance or unease, when one night Mrs Chapman, going into the Oak Room, saw a female figure standing by one of the windows. She was young, with dark hair falling over her shoulders, and was dressed in a silk petticoat over which was a white robe. She was gazing intently through the window as if looking for someone. As Mrs Chapman rubbed her eyes in astonishment at what she saw, the figure vanished. Shortly afterwards, when she had gone downstairs, one of the servants came to her in a great state of panic, saying she had just seen a terribly ugly old woman looking in at her through the lobby window. The girl was trembling and almost crying, but Mrs Chapman, though sufficiently disturbed at what she had herself seen, thought it wiser to laugh at the girl, leading her to the lobby window, which looked out onto a locked door, assuring her that she must have imagined it all.

Soon after this the house began to have inexplicable disturbances: very loud noises waking them all up in the night, 'something like the banging of a crowbar on the outside pump', as one of the frightened maids described it. One day Mr Chapman brought a friend with him to stay the night, and when the room had been prepared, his wife thought she would go up and check that everything was as it should be for a guest. To her surprise, someone seemed to follow her up the stairs and into the room, moving towards the fireplace, but when she turned round, no one was there. She decided to say nothing about it, in case she had imagined it, and on going downstairs again she joined her husband and his friend.

After a few minutes there was a tap at the door, and a servant entered to ask if she could speak to her mistress. Mrs Chapman went out to find the servant looking quite scared and white. She said she had been up to the guest-room with a candle and matches for the night when someone followed her upstairs, into the room and towards the fireplace. Mrs Chapman managed to soothe the girl, in spite of her own disturbed mind, and the matter was dropped.

Some time after this, footsteps were heard in different parts of the house. One night she distinctly heard them coming upstairs and pausing outside her bedroom door; springing out of bed, holding a loaded pistol she always kept on a table in case of burglars, she opened the door suddenly, but there was no one there. In spite of her efforts to conceal her own fears, the evidence of something supernatural in the house was becoming increasingly evident. The servants had all heard mysterious noises while eating in the kitchen: door-latches lifted, footsteps, banging out in the courtyard.

One night, when the servant who had first told Mrs Chapman about the footsteps as she went upstairs refused to sleep alone, Mrs Chapman allowed her to sleep in her own room. Suddenly in the night she was awakened by the servant's voice crying out 'Wake me! Wake me!' in great anguish and fear. When she suddenly awoke, she told her mistress she had had a bad dream, as if she were sleeping in the Oak Room, at one end of which she saw the white figure of a young girl, with long dark hair, in an old-fashioned dress, while in another part of the room was a very ugly old woman, also in old-fashioned clothes. Then the old woman said to the young girl, 'What have you done with the child?' The girl answered, 'Oh, I did not kill it. He was preserved and grew up and joined the regiment and went to India.'

The servant paused before continuing: 'Then the girl turned to me and said, "I have never spoken to mortal before but I will tell you all. My name is Miss Black." Then the old woman interrupted her and came to me in bed and laid her hand on my shoulder, which gave me such excruciating pain that it woke me up.'

Mrs Chapman did all she could to comfort the servant, begging her to say nothing to anyone and pleading with her not to give notice, promising she would do everything in her power to help her.

The very next day she began making discreet enquiries and discovered that, some seventy or eighty years before, the house had belonged to a Mrs Ravenhall, who had a niece, Miss Black, living with her. After some time Mrs Chapman herself saw the figure of a very old woman in the Oak Room; she was wringing her hands and staring at a corner of the room. The floorboards of the area were pulled up but nothing was there.

By now both Mrs Chapman and her husband had decided they must quit the house, for the servants would no longer stay in what was obviously a haunted house. They had been there three years, and such inexplicable happenings were in no way conducive to staying another four years. In any case, there seemed no way of solving the mystery of Miss Black and the old woman.

As if that mystery were not enough, another incident followed which was more improbable still, even ludicrous, and which was to hasten their departure.

Mr and Mrs Chapman were lying in bed one night when Mrs Chapman was suddenly awakened to see a different figure altogether at the foot of the bed. It was a very dark-complexioned man dressed in working clothes, a dark-dyed, thick-twilled, short-napped cotton jacket with a red choker round his neck, not at all pleasant to look at. As she began to move, he disappeared. Mr Chapman was still sleeping and saw nothing.

A few days later, just before they were due to move, Mrs Chapman asked her husband to order some coal on his way to London, for the few remaining days. The next day she told him the coal had come, at which he seemed surprised because he told her he had forgotten to order any. She was more than puzzled and asked the servants if they knew anything, but they did not. Determined to find out what had happened, she met the coalman the next day in the village and asked him if he could explain. He told her that a dark-complexioned stranger, wearing a dark jacket and a red choker round his neck, had ordered the coal which he had delivered. Mrs Chapman and the servants saw no more apparitions before they moved.

Mr Chapman had meanwhile found a tenant eager to take over the lease. He was a clergyman who ran a small school for which the premises were ideal. But the clergyman and his pupils were unable to stay long in the house, driven out by the same disturbances and uncanny footsteps. It is even more surprising that he was unable to exorcize them, something only a priest could do with success.

The house was then empty for some years until it was finally demolished and a new one built on the spot in 1868. No sightings of any ghosts have occurred since.

One can only guess at any explanation of all the happenings in that house, and perhaps it is best to leave it an unsolved series of strange events.

Hertfordshire: *Markyate: The Highway-woman Ghost*

In the year 1878 the Victorian historian W. B. Gerish made a special pilgrimage to Markyate Cell in the village of Markyate, not far from today's Whipsnade Zoo, to make a personal investigation of that splendid mansion which had for over a century belonged to the distinguished Ferrers family. Mr Gerish's visit was occasioned by a serious fire that had destroyed part of it. The owner, a Mr Adey, was anxious to repair the damage but had found it impossible to persuade any local labour even to consider entering a house reputedly badly haunted. He had therefore been obliged to engage labourers from London who had no knowledge of its history, much less its ghost.

Mr Gerish found on his arrival that work had begun to re-open a bricked-up doorway which had been revealed by the fire. It was discovered that the door opened onto a narrow stone staircase leading to a secret chamber. News of this had quickly spread through the village and round the countryside, reviving the long-forgotten legend of the 'wicked' Lady Ferrers. Mr Gerish was soon inundated with rumours and stories handed down of her evil exploits as a highway robber and of her amassed and undiscovered plunder buried in the grounds, or perhaps even in the now discovered secret chamber. He heard stories of sounds being heard and of sightings of her ghost wandering about, which, as a historian and investigator of the supernatural, he was deeply interested to examine during the three days he was to stay before making his report.

Markyate Cell had been so named after a cell or hermitage occupied in 1119 by a Benedictine monk of St Albans. On the site of this cell the present splendid mansion was built by Humphrey Bourchier, who had been granted the estate by Henry VIII after the Dissolution of the Monasteries. Upon his death, his wife Elizabeth married George Ferrers, who was a great favourite of Edward VI, a member of Lincoln's Inn and MP for Plymouth. The manor and mansion remained in the Ferrers family for over a century from that time. It stands on the east side of Watling Street, north of the village of Markyate.

Sir George Ferrers had a son, Knighton Ferrers of Bayford, Hertfordshire, who married Katherine, Second daughter and co-heir of Sir William Walton of Wimbledon, Surrey. They had a daughter Catherine, the 'wicked' Lady Ferrers. (It has been essential to make a thorough search of these genealogical details because of the continuous inaccuracies of dates and names in all the articles written on Lady Ferrers. The author and his wife, after many hours of research have been given accurate details by the Archivist of Hertfordshire County Council, who gave extracts from Clutterbuck's *History and Antiquities of Hertfordshire*, 1815-27.)

In the year 1640, when Catherine was six years old, her father died; not long after, her grandfather died, the two being buried in the same grave at Flamstead. This left Catherine sole heiress to the Ferrers estates, obviously attracting many suitors. Her mother remarried Simon Fanshawe of that most distinguished family, going back to Edward III; John Fanshawe was Remembrancer and MP for the Cinque Port of Rye during the reign of Elizabeth I, when he also purchased Ware Park in Hertfordshire. He had married Mary Bourchier, so that the Ferrers and the Fanshawes were more than just neighbours at that time.

Simon Fanshawe, by marrying Catherine's mother, was not slow to recognize the possibility of strengthening the bond between his family and the orphaned Catherine, more so because the second Civil War had broken out and they were, as Royalists, becoming more and more impecunious as the Parliamentary victories increased. Thus it came about that, when Catherine was only fourteen, Simon Fanshawe's nephew Thomas (who later became Second Viscount Fanshawe of Ware), possibly sixteen years old, married her in 1648, the year before Charles I was executed.

The marriage of two children, as they were, was not abnormal in those times, and the dowry brought by the bride was automatically and legally the property of the bridegroom. The administration of Catherine's affairs was another matter, and Simon Fanshawe appointed an unscrupulous lawyer named Joshua Lomax to conduct all the business to enable the Ferrers fortune to pass to the Fanshawes. Once this was accomplished, the young Thomas left Catherine in the lurch. There has been much speculation about his character, whether he was a brute to his child wife or not, but something very serious must have occurred to embitter Catherine, so that for the rest of her short life she took up the risks of a highway robber. The house at least was hers, and for a few years she came under the guardianship of a Lady Bedell.

Legend then takes over and says she came under the influence of a neighbouring farmer named Ralph Chaplin, who increased his income by becoming a highwayman, as so many men did in those times, notably two of the Verney family at Tring, who were forced to spend a small fortune to save them from the gallows and dishonour of the family. The proximity of Watling Street to Markyate Cell along which coaches constantly travelled from London to the North and back again meant that wealthy ladies and gentlemen were always passing.

For whatever reason, the beautiful young Catherine first dressed up as a highwayman and started her life of daring and dangerous activity; she seems to have been even more skilful than the highwaymen. She rode a magnificent jet-black horse with white feet, named Striker, and had obviously learned to be a good shot as well as a rider. The quality of her fine clothes increased with the plunder she relieved from rich travellers, who were obliged to 'stand and deliver', that cry dreaded by all travellers on the roads in those times.

It must have been at the beginning of this new and dangerous life that she discovered and decided to use the secret chamber revealed two centuries later by the fire, from which she could slip out to the courtyard stables and on to Watling Street without ever being seen. She is also said to have had another hide-out at the Pot Inn at Gustard Wood, where it was firmly believed, after her death, that she had hidden much of her loot, though none was ever discovered. Her exploits became notorious, though her identity was unknown. Markyate seemed suddenly to have become a noted spot for a highwayman.

Inevitably, with such a momentum of successes, Lady Ferrers' excitement grew even more and led to her last exploit. A wagon travelling from London with supplies for the Pot Inn, her supposed hide-out near Wheathampstead, had hidden amongst the goods two men whom the driver had picked up along the road. The wagon had begun to cross Normansland Common near St Albans when suddenly, silently and with great speed they were confronted by a masked highwayman demanding that they 'stand and deliver'. On their refusal, the driver was shot dead without warning or mercy. At the same moment one of the hidden men managed to fire back and saw the highwayman slump in the saddle, then swiftly race away into the darkness on what was to be the last ride of Lady Ferrers and this time without any plunder.

Early the next morning a servant found the body of his mistress, dressed in a highwayman's clothes, blood still dripping from a bullet wound in her right shoulder. Later her horse was also found, blood all over its saddlecloth, never before recognized as the animal used for highway robbery.

Silently and at night Lady Ferrers' body was transported across the county and buried in the parish church of St Mary the Virgin, Ware, on 13 June 1660. She had been aged only twenty-six.

The Civil Wars were over. Cromwell was dead and the Restoration began with Charles II's being crowned King, but the legend of the 'wicked' Lady Ferrers lives on in the legends of Hertfordshire and far beyond.

Was her decision to become a highwaywoman a revenge against her treatment by her husband, or against 'society', or as a woman scorned or with a deranged mind, or simply a desire for a life of daring, danger and crime? None of these questions will ever be answered. Her ghost has never ceased to haunt Markyate Cell. Long after her death she was seen wandering round the grounds and the local roads, in the woods near her hide-out in Wheathampstead and, quite unaccountably, swinging in the wind from the branches of a sycamore tree underneath which her treasure was supposed to be buried. She has even been seen mounted on Striker galloping along the road and leaping over the treetops, as secret and silent as she was throughout her life.

London: *A London Trio*

The Hummums

A number of ghost stories, well documented and witnessed, concern those who appear to dying relatives, but some appear at the very moment of death to friends. A classic example is the apparition of Myles Peter Andrews to Lord Lyttelton, as described in my earlier book, *Britain's Haunted Heritage*. Such a case happened in connexion with the Hummums, considered by Dr Samuel Johnson 'the best accredited ghost story he had ever heard', as he told his famous biographer James Boswell. This boast is very questionable and was probably expressed because the apparition was a relative of the Doctor. The story, as reported in Boswell's *Life of Johnson*, is very slight but quite singular.

The Hummums (the name derived from the Turkish *hamam*, a bath) were two late-eighteenth-century hotels near each other in the south-east corner of the old Covent Garden market. One was the *old* Hummums, the other the *new* Hummums, both of them having the then popular and fashionable Turkish baths. As in the East, they attracted wealthy patrons as well as the more dissolute members of the public, who brought with them intrigue, gossip and slander, together with immoral desires and needs not to be satisfied in other hotels that were more respectable.

The *old* Hummums were those connected with Dr Johnson. The apparition was a Mr Ford, known widely as a profligate parson, painted in Hogarth's *Midnight Modern Conversation*.

Boswell and the learned Doctor were exchanging conversation at Mr Thrale's house in Streatham, where they were constant guests, especially of Mrs Thrale. There were numerous prints of Hogarth's paintings on the walls, which prompted Boswell to ask the Doctor if there were any truth in the story he had heard in one of the Hummums of 'the riotous and notorious parson portrayed in the print'. He was emphatically assured that what he had heard was indeed the truth: 'He had purchased a living in the country, but not simoniacally. I never saw him but in the country. I have been told he was a man of great parts; very profligate, but I never heard he was impious.'

The story of Ford's ghost was that a waiter at the Hummums, who had been absent for some time, had returned knowing nothing of Ford's death, which had occurred while he was away, but, going down to the cellar, his first duty, he met Ford. He met him again when he went down a second time. When he came up again, he asked some people of the house if they knew why Ford was down in the cellar, as he had never seen him there before and wondered if anything was wrong, or was he looking for anything in particular? To his astonishment, they told him Ford was dead.

So great was the shock that the waiter became ill and continued so for some time. After his recovery he told one of the other members of the staff that he had been given a message by Ford, which he was to deliver to some women, but he was forbidden to pass it on to anyone else and had given his word of honour to keep the matter a secret. He walked out on his errand, oblivious of the fact that one of the other men was following him, continuing to do so until they came somewhere near St Paul's, where he lost Ford. When the waiter returned from his mission, he said he had delivered the message and that the women had cried, 'Then we are all undone!'

Dr Pellet, sceptical and somewhat dubious about anything dealing with the supernatural, decided to examine the truth of Ford's story. After a thorough investigation, he found the evidence irrefutable but gave no reason for this. Dr Johnson, however, summed it all up in his own way when he told Boswell: 'My wife went to the Hummums (it is a place where people get themselves cupped). I believe she went with the intention to hear about this story of Ford. At first they were unwilling to tell her; but after they had talked to her she came away satisfied that it was true. To be sure the man had a fever, and this vision may have been the beginning of it. But if the message to the women, and their behaviour upon it, were true as related, there was something supernatural. That rests upon his word, and there it remains.'

The Haunted House

A remarkable apparition was that of the son of Lord Mohun, as told by John Aubrey. He, like Dr Johnson's wife, checked the story to prove the truth.

In the year 1647, two years before the execution of Charles I, a bitter quarrel broke out between Lord Mohun's son and a Prince Griffin, resulting in a challenge to a duel being given, to take place in Chelsea Fields, with swords and on horseback. At ten o'clock on the morning of the contest young Mohun was on his way to the meeting-place when, as he reached Ebury Farm, he fell into an ambush laid by men probably paid by Griffin. He was savagely attacked and killed. Griffin knew Mohun to be a fine duellist and a better horseman, whereas he was not very good at either but had had to accept the challenge.

At that precise time 'a handsome woman, but common', living in King Street, Covent Garden, who had 'known' Mohun, saw his apparition come into her room, pull her bed-curtains aside and stand looking at her in silence, then disappear. She at once called out for help to a maid who had a key to her room, but she had seen nothing. In fact, the door had been securely locked after her mistress had gone to bed.

John Aubrey himself had the story he had been told investigated by a friend, who confirmed that every detail of it was true and that it must have been a supernatural visitation.

From that time the house had a reputation for being haunted; in a part of London not noted for its respectability, it became unfortunate for the usual flourishing 'business'. A surveyor, called in to inspect the old house, discovered that the cellar was almost full of coal and, as he wished to examine the wall behind, he was forced to take a nearby shovel to clear a path. When he returned upstairs, he warned the housekeeper, who had been there for years, about the dangerous steps down to the cellar and the mass of coal. The man said he knew nothing about steps or coal. Later, when the surveyor returned to check measurements, he found on reaching the cellar that there was no coal there at all. Returning upstairs, he saw a manservant who, after listening to his story, told him that servant after servant had left because of the terrible fear they had experienced of 'something' in the cellar. He himself had once taken a revolver down and fired a shot at a figure that had vanished as he fired. The house was so haunted that no one would stay there at night, and so business had declined for some of the occupants.

Field of the Forty Footsteps

In the late eighteenth century two important magazines published accounts of a haunted plot of ground in the middle of a field that for many years lay barren. Southampton Fields were at that time behind where the British Museum now is, at the extreme north-east of Upper Montague Street, and were a well-known place for fighting duels. No grass would ever grow over the bare ground, which defeated every effort to replant it and which was avoided by countless people, day and night. The haunted patch of bare ground became widely known as 'the Field of the Forty Footsteps'.

The particular duel which gave its name to the Field of the Forty Footsteps was not reported until the reign of George III by the *Gentleman's Magazine*, on 17 July 1778, and the opposite side of the account in the *Arminian Magazine* for 1781. The latter headed its account 'The Brothers' Steps' and dealt with it more briefly than the former magazine.

The extraordinary fact is that the duel giving the place its name happened during the reign of James II, when, within six months of that king's accession to the throne in 1685, James, Duke of Monmouth, illegitimate son of Charles II by Lucy Walter, landed at Lyme in Dorset, where he was proclaimed king by the Protestants and led 'the Monmouth Rebellion'. The duel took place between two unnamed brothers who fought on different sides in the Monmouth Rebellion, and who, because of a quarrel over 'a worthless woman', finished by their killing each other. According to the *Arminian Magazine*: 'the prints of their feet are about the depth of three inches, and nothing will vegetate, so much as to disfigure them. The number is only eighty-three but probably some at present are filled up. For I think there were formerly more in the centre, where each unhappy combatant wounded the other to death. And a bank on which the first fell retains the form of his agonizing couch by the curse of barrenness, while grass flourished all about it.'

The *Gentleman's Magazine* states the following, but it is well to note that the mention of Charles II and the earlier date of 1686 are serious inaccuracies; otherwise the account is much more interesting.

The print of their feet is near three inches in depth, and remains totally barren; so much so that nothing will grow to disfigure them. Their number I did not reckon but suppose they may be about ninety. A bank on which the first fell, who was mortally wounded and died on the spot, retains the form of his agonising posture by the curse of barrenness while the grass grows round it. A friend of mine showed me these steps in the year 1760, when he could trace them back by old people to the year 1686; but it was generally supposed to have happened in the early part of the reign of Charles II. There are people now living who well remember their being ploughed up, and barley sown to deface them; but all was labour in vain; for the prints returned in a short time to their original form. There is one thing I nearly forgot to mention: that a place on the bank is still to be seen where, tradition says, the wretched woman sat to see the combat. I am sorry I can throw no more light on the subject; but am convinced in my opinion that the Almighty has ordered it as a standing monument of His just displeasure of the horrid sin of duelling.

The Field of the Forty Footsteps has long been built over and may well have formed part of the site of the British Museum, which has more than enough of its own hauntings to worry about the Southampton Fields of long ago. There is still no record of the names of the brothers or of the place where they were buried.

4 The North

Cheshire: *Altrincham: The White Lady of Ashley Hall*

All that now remains of the once splendid seventeenth-century mansion Ashley Hall is, according to Pevsner, a large forecourt of farm buildings, one of them impressive, long, with pedimented wings and doorcase; it was once served by a railway station between Knutsford and Altrincham.

Ashley Hall has always been renowned for its ghost of a White Lady, whose existence as a once real person has never been identified, nor indeed the reason for her constant haunting of one room, known as 'the Cedar Room', of all the many rooms in the rambling old mansion.

On 2 May 1906 *The Cheshire Sheaf* published the following, which in itself might well have been a quotation from a trade almanac: 'Who the White Lady was is a mystery. All that is known with certainty is that she haunts a room known as the "Cedar Room" in Ashley Hall, a Cheshire mansion pleasantly situated on the banks of the Bollen, rather more than a mile south-east of Bowdon. The frights she has given, the illnesses she has caused, the speculations to which she has given rise would fill a volume. S.J.C.'

T.A. Coward in his *Cheshire, Traditions and History, 1932* states: 'Ashley Hall had its orthodox ghost, a white lady, but she seems to have retired and never shows herself now, though I remember cab-men who affirmed that they had seen her.' This seems improbable evidence, since she is known to confine her hauntings to the Cedar Room, surely not visited by taxi-drivers!

The origin of this ghost first appeared in T. Otway's book *News from the Invisible World*, published in 1836 according to the British Museum catalogue, its story supposedly having been related to him by someone in Cambridge University and finally repeated by Ingram.

Even more confusing than the ghost are the names of the owners of Ashley Hall given in versions of the story. The Breretons and the Merediths, two ancient families, certainly were the owners at one time. Ingram, presumably quoting Otway, gives the names of the principals as Mrs Mannering, her daughter, her daughter's intimate friend and Mrs Mannering's sister, Lady Pierrepoint. Ingram was a scholarly and highly authoritative writer on the supernatural; one would want considerable proof to dispute him, as has been done in a recent paraphrase. His description of Mrs Mannering, presumably from Otway, is in itself intriguing, since she is the principal in the story.

Mrs Mannering was a widow, blessed with an ample fortune and great animal spirits, who laughed, ate, talked and played the kind hostess, delighting in seeing everyone happy about her. She thanked God that she had not a nerve in her body and hoped that she would die as she had lived – comfortably. These attributes do not seem to be justified at the end of the story of the White Lady; indeed, they add to the whole mystery.

The story was related by a young girl who had just left school and was invited by her friend Miss Mannering to stay at Ashley Hall, where her mother was the then owner. Upon their arrival they found that the Hall was crowded with guests; after many apologies, Mrs Mannering said there was only one room, used as an ante-room and known as 'the Cedar Room' because of its being wainscoted with cedar, which the girl could have. There was dancing after dinner, and it was between the hours of two and three o'clock in the morning that the girl went to bed. The Cedar Room was quite obviously an ante-room and not a bedroom, though a hurriedly made bed had been put in there while she was at dinner. There was no other furniture, no old pictures or tapestries on the walls, as one might have expected in a very old mansion. There were two doors leading out to passages and other rooms, an empty fireplace and sashed windows.

After securely locking both doors and windows and falling asleep, she was awakened by the sight of a female figure moving slowly and noiselessly through the room and disappearing through the locked door. Strangely enough, she felt no alarm, thinking that perhaps a guest had lost her way in the labyrinth of passages and rooms of the Hall, and she went to sleep again. In the morning, before going down to breakfast, she was surprised to find that the doors she had locked the previous night were still firmly locked.

At breakfast Mrs Mannering asked her if she had slept well, but when asked who the lady was who had been in the room last night, she made no answer, only looked at the girl with earnestness, seemed on the point of answering, checked herself and remained silent.

The next night the girl went to bed early, and at the same hour as on the previous night she awoke to see the same figure moving past her bed. This time she had no doubt, for she plainly saw its face, pale and drawn, with large, black, melancholy eyes, as the figure moved noiselessly across the room and back again, stopping dead in the middle. In terror the girl watched it, unable to move. Then suddenly it vanished. The rest of the night she remained sleepless, shocked and frightened, determined to end her visit early the next morning.

Mrs Mannering was not at breakfast, as excitement filled the house with plans for the race ball to be held the next evening. The day was bright, with a cloudless sky, so that the girl decided to stay one more night. All through the day she was unable to forget what she had seen in the Cedar Room. She sang, she played, she did everything to avoid going to bed till long after the dreaded hour of two had passed. When she did go up to bed, she made a thorough investigation of the room, every corner of it, testing and re-testing the door, locks and window sashes. With a beating heart, she went uneasily to bed, in an agony of fear of what might happen, unable to sleep until in exhaustion she must have dozed off. When her eyes opened, it was dawn and, glad the night had passed, she rose in her bed, then fell back at the sight of the white figure, this time bending right over, so near that she could have touched it, the white drapery the figure wore almost falling over the girl, before she fainted.

It was noon before she recovered. The servants and indeed Mrs Mannering herself had all knocked on the door to wake her, before deciding it would be better not to disturb her. Rising, she found Mrs Mannering in the breakfast room about to rally her on her lateness, but she was checked by the girl's appearance, asking her if she were well. Her guest replied that she was very far from feeling well and that she would not stay in the house any longer. Mrs Mannering then asked if she had any particular reason for leaving. Receiving an account of all that had happened, she listened carefully without interrupting, before confessing that she herself had heard strange noises and that friends had told strange tales which she was sure were idle fancies. Then suddenly she said: 'But for God's sake don't mention it. Assure me. Promise you will not breathe a syllable on the subject to any living being. If, among these ignorant and superstitious people, the inexplicable occurrence should once get wind, not a servant would stay with me.' Though assured that her room would be changed, the girl remained firm about going and left the Hall that morning.

After a long interval, during which time Miss Mannering had died, her friend accepted another invitation to come to Ashley Hall, since Mrs Mannering's letter was personal and pressing. Upon her arrival she found that her hostess's sister, Lady Pierrepoint, and her three children had also been invited and was astonished that the mother insisted on the three children being put in the Cedar Room, in spite of all Mrs Mannering's pleas not to put them there. Lady Pierrepoint was described by her husband Richard as having 'an unparalleled tongue', as was evident from her insistent answers to Mrs Mannering.

Mrs Mannering said the children would be cold. Her ladyship said she wished them to be hardy. 'It was out of the way.' 'So much the better. Their noise would not be troublesome.' 'I fear ...,' began Mrs Mannering. 'Don't know what it is,' answered her ladyship. Mrs Mannering gave in and the children moved into the haunted room, '...together with their cribs and rocking horses, nurses and nine-pins, formally established in the dreaded apartment', as the girl narrated.

Everything went smoothly for a fortnight, to her surprise, remembering what her experiences had been. Mrs Mannering was herself quite happy until one morning, when she went into the Cedar Room, she found the children packing up all their toys.

'What, are you tired of Ashley, and going to leave me?' she asked.

'Oh, no; but we are going to hide away our toys from the White Lady. She came last night, and Sunday night. And she had such large black eyes, and she stood close by our cribs – just here, aunt. Who is she, do you know? for Fred says she never speaks. What does she do here, and what does she want?'

'What a wretched, miserable woman I am!' cried the panic-stricken Mrs Mannering. 'Every hope I had entertained of this abominable affair is dashed to the ground for ever; and if, by any chance, Lady Pierrepoint should discover – Oh, they must be moved directly. Ring the bell! Where's the housekeeper? I'll give no reason – I'll *have* no reason. Oh, Mannering! to what sorrows have you not exposed your widow!'

In spite of all inquiries, interrogatories, and surmises, moved the little Pierrepoints were that very evening.

In spite of this, the children brought up the subject again at dinner, when one of them said, 'Mamma, I've something to tell you about the White Lady.' The children were then bundled out of the room, but the story-teller goes on: 'I shall never forget the piteous expression of Mrs Mannering's countenance, as she passed me with her party, or her declaration: "God forgive me! but I see very clearly this White Lady will put me in my grave." ' The room was then shut up for many years and no account of what passed at Ashley in the interim was known.

The last time this friend was invited to Ashley was for the celebrations of the coming-of-age of young Mannering; after she has given a description of the party, the presentation of the tenants to him and later the more distinguished guests, she tells how Mrs Mannering went up to change in the Cedar Room. (It had been returned to use as an ante-room.) Throwing off her shawl and bonnet, she ran hastily to a swing glass which stood near a window. She was adjusting her dress when, looking up for a moment, she was confronted by the White Lady in the glass. Her collapse and fall with her terror of the apparition resulted in brain-fever and, after some days, in her death.

The last report about this unsolved mystery of the ghost of Ashley Hall was in 1961 in *Cheshire Village Memories*, compiled by the Cheshire Federation of Women's Institutes, kindly pointed out to me by Mr Peter Bamford, Chester Reference Librarian, to whom I am greatly indebted. 'The Hall also has a ghost, the White Lady, but of late her spirit seems to have moved on, though her footsteps are still sometimes heard.' These steps add even more to the mystery of the ghost, for she was only seen and moved noiselessly, according to the story related by Ingram.

Derbyshire: *Eyam, near Chapel-en-le-Frith: The Haunted Murder Stone*

On Wednesday evening, 18 July 1823, one of the most callous and barbarous murders in the criminal history of Derbyshire was committed on a lonely road between Whaley Bridge, on the edge of the county, and Disley in Cheshire.

The murdered man was William Wood, thirty years old, who had lived at Eyam and left a widow and three children. His body was first seen by Edmund Pott, a labourer, and his companion, John Mellor, who lived at Kettlehulme, who were returning home from Stockport with their cart and horses when ahead of them they suddenly saw a crumpled shape half lying on the grass bank on the edge of the road. As they stopped, they saw, with fear and horror, that it was a man's body, still warm, blood flowing from the crushed and battered head. He could have been dead only a few minutes. The head lay on bloodstained stones, some of them still having hair on them; one of them, oblong, with bloodstained finger-marks, had obviously been used to batter the skull deep into the grass. Tenderly the two men lifted the corpse into their cart, the blood still flowing, as well as some of the bloodstained stones, especially the oblong one. They then set off to Whaley Bridge, where they deposited the corpse in the Cock Inn to await the coroner.

So violent was the method of the murder that the spot where it took place was haunted for many years. Such was the feeling in the surrounding countryside that no one dared go near it, even by day. Those forced to use the road and brave enough to do so reported that the ground remained barren, that no grass ever grew there and that the deep cavity caused by the battered skull remained amidst the bloodstained stones. All efforts to fill the cavity failed, for every time the stones were unaccountably removed.

On the following Saturday the inquest was held, and the two men acted as principal witnesses, relating in detail the horrific wounds they had seen and identifying the exhibited bloodstained stones they had brought with them to the Cock Inn shortly after. Another witness gave evidence of having seen three men running away from the vicinity of the murder; slowing to a walk, they had asked how far it was to Chapel-en-le Frith; when told 'Four miles', they at once began running again until out of sight. The witness was able to say that they were all young men, one of them taller than the other two, wearing a jean jacket and trousers. One of the others had a blood streak on his shoulder about five inches long. The jury returned a verdict of wilful murder by a person or persons unknown. The whole proceedings were published in the *Derby Mercury* on 23 July 1823.

It appears that William Wood, a small cloth-manufacturer, had been to Manchester to sell his goods, receiving a bill of exchange for £60 and notes for £10 for the total sale. He had cashed the bill in Stockport, and in both cases the numbers of the notes were registered by the cashiers, a matter of vital importance in tracking down and arresting at least two of the murderers. According to one of them, Charles Taylor, who was quickly caught and made a full confession, he and two others, whom he named, had met Wood on his way home from Chapel-en-le Frith to Eyam. He had invited them to a pub to have a drink. He seemed to have a lot of money, and they decided to follow and rob him. It was probably because Wood put up a desperate fight that he was murdered.

On the day of the inquest, Saturday 19 July 1823, a neighbouring paper, the *Macclesfield Courier*, reported:

On Thursday morning, three young men, two rather shabbily dressed, and the third in a new fustian jacket and trowsers, came into this town [Macclesfield] and went to the Golden Lion public-house. The younger of the three then proceeded to Mr Burgess's in Chestergate, and purchased three complete suits of cloathes, he also bought shoes, &c. from Mr Wainwright, in the same street, and then returned to his companions, who stated they were related to Mr David Browne, and wished to change their cloathes before they saw him. Having done so, they had some beef steaks, &c. and left the house, one of them leaving his old cloathes behind him. The youngest of the three then went into Chestergate, and offered the remainder of their old things to two lads carrying in coals for Mr Wainwright, who accepted of them: they then proceeded by the Telegraph coach to Manchester. Shortly afterwards, intelligence of the murder having reached Macclesfield, a suspicion arose that these three fellows had been concerned in the deed, and upon examining their old cloathes, they were found much stained with blood. Mr Frost, the constable, immediately proceeded to Manchester by the Mail – We have seen the cloathes of these men, they are much smeared with dirt, (evidently from a *lime* road,) to conceal the blood on them, which in many places is very visible in the inside, and we have not the smallest doubt that the owners of them are the perpetrators of the bloody deed.

In Manchester the three young men were observed in the Greyhound public house in Oak Street. The landlord, recognizing them from the day before and noticing they were now smartly dressed, was suspicious that they were robbers and sent his son to the police office. When two of the officers came to the inn, there was only one man there, whom they closely questioned. As he seemed to have information of great value, he was taken into custody for further investigation. It was found that he had spent six months imprisoned in Chester Castle for felony and had been released only the day before the murder. He was removed to the New Bailey prison to await trial on a charge of murder, following a full confession he had made. He was named Taylor, and he named the others as Platt and Dale, declaring that Platt was the actual murderer and that he himself had played no part in it, other than having been there. That same night, in his cell, he made a rope of his stockings and garters and attempted to hang himself but was discovered and cut down. The wounds inflicted, however, were too severe and he died shortly after. He was about twenty years old. All this was reported in the *Manchester Mercury* on 22 July 1823.

The police were now able to circulate a description of the other two, as given them by Taylor. An intensive search was at once made for them, and they were nearly caught together in Manchester, last seen running across fields and out of sight. On 9 August Dale was arrested as a result of the full description given by Taylor. He had apparently turned up at Liverpool and gone into a recruiting office to join up, perhaps hoping to evade capture by being sent abroad. The recruiting officer, however, at once informed the Cheshire police, and Dale was arrested. He was sent for trial at Chester Assizes. The police, though, came under bitter attack from the press for what was considered culpable negligence, as no attempt had been made to offer a reward for any capture, for their inability to find Platt and because the main work had been carried out by the Manchester constables.

Dale, though only seventeen years of age, was a curiously complex character, the son of a 'doting mother' who lived in Manchester; he had twice previously been convicted of felony. Dale accused Platt of having done the actual murder, stating that he had only received 4s. 6d. for keeping watch while it was taking place. This was a downright lie, for he had had some of the numbered notes on him when arrested, charged with the murder of William Wood. During the trial, a Cheshire newspaper, in a leading article, castigated the prisoner for appearing '...dressed in a fashionable cut coat, pantaloons, and silk stockings, thickly starched shirt collar as high as his ears, and his hair turned back à la Brutus'.

The jury brought in a verdict of guilty. Although the sentence was deferred on a technical count brought by defending counsel, a consultation by twelve judges upheld the original verdict. Sentence of death was accordingly passed, the execution to take place on 21 April 1824. During his detention nineteen-year-old Dale's health had sharply deteriorated. He had also 'become religious', as was reported in one of the newspapers, which stated that, 'Within the last few years, a set of young maudlin Philanthropists, and Evangelical Damsels' had sought to save the souls of men convicted of murder and sentenced to death.

It was quite probably such a religious group who put up the stone memorial, known as 'the Murder Stone', on the fiftieth anniversary year of Dale's execution, which is still standing at the roadside on the road from Whaley Bridge to Disley, above the very spot where William Wood was murdered. It is inscribed thus:

WILLIAM WOOD
EYAM, DERBYSHIRE
HERE
MURDERED
JULY 16th
AD 1823
Prepare to meet thy God

On the night previous to Dale's execution he ate his supper apparently with a good appetite. It was with much difficulty that his gaoler persuaded him to rest. He at last consented and slept soundly for three hours. When making his final confession, he stated that Platt's real name was Brett, which may well have helped him to avoid arrest. For breakfast on the morning of the execution he drank two cups of tea and ate an egg and some toast, after which he smoked a pipe or two of tobacco, but he was most anxious for the arrival of the City Sheriff. A splendid gold ring he was earlier wearing was not seen at the execution. After receiving the Holy Sacrament he was led out to the scaffold.

Of Dale's guilt there can be no doubt, for in his final confession he stated that he had been present on the watch whilst Taylor and Brett perpetrated the murder. He said he had called out to them not to kill the man, and he had previously expressed his contrition for the share he had in the crime. He was executed at five o'clock in the morning before a crowd of about 300. After the body had hung for an hour, it was cut down and handed to the surgeons for dissection.

The hour of his execution was severely criticized by the local press as being far too early. Had it taken place at lunch-time, several thousand people would have assembled to witness it, at what the paper described as 'a more civilised hour'.

In 1859 Alfred Fryer, author of *Wilmslow Graves*, during his researches visited the spot. (He may well have called at Tunstead Farm, not far away, in search of the most delightful and bewitching skull of 'Dickie', ruling over that part of Derbyshire, described in my book *Britain's Haunted Heritage*.) Fryer investigated the legend of the barren ground at Eyam where no grass grew, together with the exposed cavity, which he described as being sixteen inches in diameter and four inches deep, 'completely free from vegetation and with nothing in its surroundings or position to protect it from being silted up after the first heavy shower'. Several local people told him of unsuccessful attempts to fill it up. John Fox told him he had once packed it full of stones very carefully, stamping down grass turves to hide it. The very next morning the turves and stones had been flung out in all directions, leaving the gaping cavity as before. He said that such 'happenings' had gone on for more than thirty years, to his knowledge. Fryer himself tried and failed to fill the hole, leaving it as he found it, considering there must be 'some physical reason hitherto unexplained'.

Lancashire: Smithills Hall, Bolton: The Bloody Footstep

On 16 April 1983 Bolton's *Evening News* published a puzzling snapshot of two children in front of an old coach belonging to Smithills Coaching House, in which a ghost was sitting. It did nothing to convince many people in Bolton, least of all the Director of Education and Arts, of its authenticity, in spite of the fact that a local historian assumed the ghost to be that of the famous martyr George Marsh, because he was wearing a clerical collar. For three centuries his bloody footstep in Smithills had inspired one of the great legends of Lancashire.

An even more unconvincing account of the martyr's footstep was given by the great American author Nathaniel Hawthorne, who once stayed at Smithills Hall and was so intensely impressed by the bloody footstep legend that he made it the basis of his novel *Septimius*, though his imagination ran away with the truth of what he had himself seen:

> On the threshold of one of the doors of Smithills Hall there is a bloody footstep impressed into the doorstep, and ruddy as if the bloody foot had just trodden there; and it is averred that, on a certain night of the year, and at a certain hour of the night, if you go and look at the door-step you will see the mark wet with fresh blood. Some have pretended to say that this appearance of blood was but dew; but can dew redden a cambric handkerchief? Will it crimson the fingertips when you touch it. And that is what the bloody footstep will surely do when the appointed night and hour come round ...

The present form of Smithills Hall was built in the reign of Henry VII by Andrew Barton, whose rebus, a tun and a bar, is carved on the walls. It is a priceless heirloom of black-and-white architecture, possibly the finest example of its kind in Lancashire. It was originally erected in 569 as a Saxon palace and thereafter inhabited by a succession of notable families, such as the Bartons, Radcliffes and Byrons. Its fame arose, however, during the reign of 'Bloody' Queen Mary (1553-8), when Sir Roger Barton, magistrate, was the owner of the house. He was a devout Catholic before whom George Marsh, a Calvinist minister, appeared to answer for his Protestant faith. The year was 1555, and legend has it that Sir Roger Barton was as much a bigot as the Queen, 'a monarch of sombre memory', as one historian described her. She was ruthless with Protestants, as was her half-sister Elizabeth with Catholics in the years when the charge of heresy led inevitably to burning at the stake.

George Marsh was one of these martyrs. He was born in 1515 in the parish of Deane, one mile from Bolton. His parents were farmers, and he was put to the plough. Quite early he was profoundly impressed with Tyndale's translation of the New Testament from the Greek, which had reached into the hearts of thousands of English people for the very first time in its history. Tyndale himself was burned at the stake. Marsh married at twenty-five but after his wife's death, 'being desirous of godly studies', went to Cambridge, then a strong Puritan university. Upon completing his studies, he soon gained the reputation of being a persuasive preacher and travelled all over the country.

After a short reign, Edward VI died and 'Bloody' Mary ascended the throne. 'The Protestants were at her feet and she struck without mercy,' wrote one historian. In her very first year George Marsh was apprehended and imprisoned as an eminent Protestant, 'for preaching false doctrines', and summoned to Smithills Hall before Barton, the magistrate.

His preliminary trial, for such it was, took place in an upper room known as 'the Green Chamber', before Sir Roger Barton and his 'Mass priest', who accompanied him. The trial was fully reported at length. There was considerable 'browbeating' by both men, and it concluded with Marsh being ordered to go for further examination by Edward, third Earl of Derby, at Latton House in West Lancashire.

A visitor to Smithills Hall in 1787 wrote the following account: 'It is said that Marsh being provoked by their taunts and provocations, on descending the stairs from the chamber, he stamped with his foot upon a stone, and looking up to heaven appealed to God for the justice of his cause, and prayed that there might in that place remain a constant memorial of the wickedness and injustice of his enemies; and it is pretended that, from that time to the present, there has remained the print of a man's foot, notwithstanding every endeavour to efface the impression.'

His prayer has been answered, for, to this very day, the impression of his foot has remained, not only in legend but in fact. It is known as 'the Bloody Footstep'. In the passage leading to the chapel of Smithills Hall it may be seen, and has been seen by countless thousands of people, upon the time-worn stone pavement. On a wall tablet are inscribed the words: 'Footprint of the Reverend George Marsh of Deane, Martyr ...'. The stone is carefully preserved by being encased in an ornamental iron covering with a hinged lid.

Almost immediately the legends began of the haunting of Smithills by George Marsh and the bloody footstep, particularly by the stone on which the footstep is. Once terrifying noises were heard throughout the Hall when it was removed. Pandemonium broke out and searches were made until it was found and put back in place, when peace reigned once more. However, there are to this day those with enquiring minds who doubt that the red imprint is real blood, but rather an admixture of ferruginous sand, which, when moisture is applied, produces a rust-coloured stain.

Marsh was treated more kindly by the Earl of Derby, being given a bed and a fire but no sympathy for his faith; he was ordered to be detained in Lancaster Castle; after further interrogation and his repeated refusal to change his religion, he was taken to Chester, where, on 24 April 1555, he was burned to death.

In that same newspaper report giving an account of a

supposed ghost in a family photograph, another suggestion was made that the ghost was not George Marsh but a Grey Lady, equally mysterious, who is supposed to haunt the restaurant of Smithills Coach House. It was first reported in 1980 by a former member of the staff. Three more customers since then have seen her, and the restaurant owner himself, whilst '...not being a great believer in the supernatural, was very puzzled by the photograph'.

The coaching house restaurant stands on the site of the Smithills Hall stables, which were burned down at the beginning of the century. The paper states that the surrounding area is full of ghosts and that one female figure has been constantly seen making almost daily journeys in the area of the farm and the Hall, which might or might not be the Grey Lady. Mysterious as all the three stories are, the Bloody Footstep takes precedence in the legends of the supernatural in Lancashire legends and folklore, and justly so; but no ghost has ever been seen in Smithills Hall, even with its reputation of being haunted.

Northumberland: *Denton Hall, near Newcastle upon Tyne: The Benevolent Ghost*

It has always been thought by the majority of people that ghosts are to be feared, that they are sinister, terrifying and unwelcome guests at any time. 'Silky' must then be very rare, for she is a kindly, caring, protective ghost, yet no one has ever been able to solve her true identity. She has been called 'Silky' throughout the centuries because she has always been seen in a rustling white silk dress, moving along passages in Denton Hall, into rooms and out into the garden. She glides rather than walks through the house, spending most of her time in two rooms, one having a curtained, four-poster bed and tall, straight-backed chairs. She is also affectionately called 'Old

Barberry', for no known reason unless it was the name of a person who countless years before had been a tenant, owner or one of the staff. Whoever the ghost is, she seems to be constantly watching over both the Hall and its occupants with special care, so that nothing unfortunate befalls.

She is, or was, venerated by all the miners in the county, who treated her as their guardian angel, since there had been times in the history of the mines when she gave warnings of accidents and disasters; mining was the main source of employment in the county, the lives of hundreds depending upon safety.

Denton Hall is 4½ miles west of Tyne Bridge on the A69 road, close to Hadrian's Wall. In fact, several of the bricks of the wall of Severus were used to build Denton Hall, which must have been erected much earlier than the extant records of the early sixteenth century. Tradition has it that the original site of the Hall was a chapel held by the monks of Tynemouth when they were lords of the whole estate, a passage having existed between the chapel and the priory. The lower of the many gardens served as a monks' cemetery. Shortly after the Reformation the property came into the possession of the Erringtons, descendants of the Dentons, and in 1780 it was held by the famous Mrs Elizabeth Montagu, who was a friend of Garrick, Goldsmith, Sir Joshua Reynolds and Dr Johnson. One of the gloomiest rooms in the Hall was known as 'Dr Johnson's Chamber'; a shady path in the garden was called 'Johnson's Walk'. Mrs Montagu was interested in 'second sight' and may well have been familiar with 'Silky's' apparition in the Hall. Dr Johnson was also interested in the occult.

There have been innumerable ghosts of warning appearing before the death of a person; sometimes warning gestures have petrified the person warned. Times out of number such warnings by ghosts have brought on death through fear; at other times they have been prophetic to the head of a house. 'Silky' has only once appeared with a warning, indicating it in silence with an outstretched arm and extended forefinger – but not threateningly, though the death of the person came shortly afterwards.

She was particularly gentle and caring when illness was in the house, constantly watching to see if the invalid was getting better. The sick person was never afraid but strangely comforted by her appearance, with watchful eyes, before vanishing. Equally noticeable were her visitations when misfortune or danger was impending. Only once did her appearance terrify: an old nurse in the Hall was prevented from entering a room by 'Silky's' figure in the doorway. Her most singular and totally inexplicable act was to enter the room of a guest at midnight and touch his hand as he lay asleep, leaving it in pain for many days afterwards.

There was only one occasion during many years that she was heard making any real noise, so silent was she in her gliding over the floors and passages of the Hall. That was when, in 1884, she was heard dragging something very heavy through two long-disused rooms, down a flight of stairs and through a closed window, found open after the noise had ceased and she had disappeared.

It has been recorded, without any evidence of the truth, that 'Silky' was the ghost of one of two sisters who long ago lived in the Hall, testimony of the story being given by an old retainer in 1894. It was said that there were two domestic servants named Ruth and Hannah Bell, one of whom dreamed that a large sum of money was buried under a flagstone in the entrance-hall; impressed by what she had dreamed, she told her sister, who betrayed her by repeating the story in the morning to their master. The master made light of the story, but that same night he found the treasure under the flagstone. Neither sister was aware of this, but a legend has been passed down relating that one sister murdered the other, the ghost being the murdered one returning to haunt the Hall and discover the treasure. It has even been suggested that 'Silky' was the victim of her jealous sister.

Immediately her apparition was seen in the Hall for the first time, watched as she moved round the garden 'at unholy hours', she became known as 'Barberry with the straw hat' and known locally as being more effectual than a bulldog for preventing children stealing apples in the orchard.

The first published account of 'Silky' appeared in Moses Richardson's *Table Book of Remarkable Occurrences*, having been told to a Mr Doubleday by the visitor to the Hall who first saw her spirit, somewhere around the year 1810. In the fullest paraphrase of this in Ingram's account, there is no doubt at all that it was 'touched up' very considerably by Thomas Doubleday, but the story gives the first evidence of 'Silky's' coming to warn someone of an impending disaster in a caring and kindly way.

Two days after being invited to the Hall, the visitor had gone with her friends to a ball being held in a neighbouring house, where she received such over-whelming attention throughout the evening from a previously slight acquaintance that a proposal of marriage was inevitable, particularly as she agreed to continue the relationship. She returned to the Hall very tired and much bewildered by what had happened and what might continue to happen. She was a rich young lady, eighteen years old, and cautious that it was not her money that attracted this suitor, as it had other men.

According to her own account to Mr Doubleday, she was sitting in an antique, winged and high-backed chair beside the fire, combing her hair and trying to sort out her thoughts about the attentions she had received at the ball, when, looking up, she saw, with more astonishment than fear, a figure sitting opposite her in a chair similar to the one she had chosen. It was an old lady who seemed to be dressed in a remarkable flowered satin gown, cut to a shape then out of date, peaked and long-waisted. The satin seemed glossy and stiff, and on her head was a strange satin hood as glossy as her dress. Her eyes were small and grey, her hands restless. Her face was not unpleasant but somewhat hard and severe; on her wrinkled fingers were rings of great size and obvious value. In a lengthy conversation the ghost warned the visitor to have nothing to do with the gentleman concerned, since his family were in such financial distress that they would shortly be ruined. The visitor sat listening intently, still with only astonishment and no fear; then suddenly the figure before her rose and glided noiselessly to the door, through which she disappeared. The visitor rose and, hurrying to the door, found it securely locked, remembering she had done so when entering the room. At breakfast next morning she recounted what she had seen. The warning that the visitor had received came true, for shortly after leaving Denton Hall she was informed of the bankruptcy, ruin and disgrace of her host of that night.

'Silky's' last appearance was recorded in the early nineteenth century, when a workman, then working in one of the passages, suddenly saw her figure approaching. He was so terrified that he fled and was ill for many weeks afterwards. Later she was seen in the dining-room, leaning meditatively against the mantelpiece, so there was surely someone in Denton Hall due to be warned of danger or who was ill and needed the care her spirit was said to bring; maybe the colliers were in danger in the pits and must have the timely warning for which they trusted her as their guardian spirit. Perhaps she just wanted to go on living in the old house she had known and loved when she was first born in, or came to, Denton Hall.

Northumberland: Black Heddon: The Malevolent Ghost

Incredible as it may seem, there was another 'Silky' not far from Denton Hall in the remote village of Black Heddon, near a tributary of the River Blyth and the charming village of Stamfordham. Unlike the benevolent Silky of Denton Hall, this ghost gave much disturbance, even fear and mystery, to the villagers. She also wore a silken and rustling dress, which gave her her name. Although Richardson, in his *Table Book of Traditions*, stated that this Silky ceased her manifold methods of annoying the inhabitants, these words were not supported by facts, for she was still haunting the village in 1840, some fifty years after Richardson's remarks.

Her vagaries and appearances were unaccountable, manifesting themselves in various ways, though she was always in her silken white costume and mostly on the roads or in the woods – a pure nature spirit, not a guardian as the other Silky was, but regarded by most of the local people as a spectral tormenter, especially to those who had to travel at night. Some of her characteristics resembled those of Madam Pigott of Chetwynd Hall in Shropshire (p. 35), for she also had a chair in a tree, out of which she would jump down on horsemen passing below, frightening the life out of them, forcing them to ride on until she chose to dismount and disappear.

Silky seems to have been obsessed by horses for some inexplicable reason, not always dropping out of a tree onto them and their riders but dogging the steps of a lone horseman compelled to travel by night. She would wait until he either entered a wood or reached a particularly dark part of the road before leaping on horse and rider, forcing them to ride on to some place she would select, then jump off and vanish, leaving the rider bewildered and terror-stricken.

At Belsay, two or three miles from Black Heddon, she had her favourite resort, a high stone crag on which she would perch, waiting for a horseman to pass, by day or night, then jump on him. There, in the twilight, the villagers had seen her ghost hewing a tree or splitting stones with a hammer, accompanied by great howls as of a terrible wind. They had seen her white phantom rushing through the woods, hair streaming, her silken dress rustling, then suddenly vanishing. At the bottom of her crag there was a lake or fishpond over which drooped a huge tree with great branches, another of her favourite haunts. She had her own chair, formed out of the division in the branches. There she would sit, rocked by the wind, enjoying it most when there was a storm. So frequently was Silky seen there that it became known as 'Silky's Seat'. It was from here that she was accused of 'meddling her worst with horses'. These animals were extraordinarily sensitive to her influence, to such an extent that her power over them was total.

One night an unfortunate farm servant was selected as her victim as he, with his horse and cart, was obliged to travel some distance to a colliery to collect coal. Silky waylaid him at a bridge as twilight fell, on the road between Black Heddon and Stamfordham, afterwards called by all the locals 'Silky's Brig'. At once, by her power, she caused the horse to come to a standstill, so that the bridge was completely blocked. Nothing could budge the horse, and the servant might have been transfixed and paralysed till dawn had not a neighbouring farm labourer happened to be approaching. The terrified carter was at last able to tell him about 'that witch Silky'. The farm labourer, who had the same fear of Silky, was always prepared for her antics by carrying witch-wood (rowan). By this charm, the power of Silky was challenged and defeated, leaving the horse to move on its journey as though nothing had happened.

Silky had more success with ploughing horses, forcing them to stop dead and not move until she released them, and in seriously confusing a hunting field – without any assistance from those who today are against all blood sports.

There had to be an end, sooner or later, to her capricious and wayward behaviour, which found no favour with the villagers, but it did not come from any action they might have taken. It was brought about by something that happened in the house of the Hepple family, responsible yeomen of the village, whose highly respectable descendants were still living there in the late nineteenth century. The abrupt disappearance of Silky after the event that happened in this house convinced almost everyone in the village that it was caused by Silky herself, who had died without revealing the secret of the whereabouts of her hidden treasure.

One day a servant maid of the Hepples was cleaning out one of the rooms when she was terror-struck by a tremendous crash above her head and the collapse of the ceiling, and narrowly escaped being killed. She ran from the room shrieking and screaming, 'The deevil's in the house! The deevil's in the house! He's come through the ceiling!'

There was consternation as the family heard the cries of fear and the collapse of the servant, so that it was a long time before any one of them dared to go into the room. Finally one, more plucky than the others, went in, only to gaze in horror at what she saw. There on the floor amidst the rubble of plaster lay a strange shape like the skin of a large black dog. It had broken open and spilled out a mass of gold.

For many years after this event the Hepples lived in great prosperity from Silky's long-hidden treasure, but she had vanished forever. According to the words of one of the Hepple descendants; 'Her destiny was accomplished, her spirit laid, and she now sleeps as peacefully and unperturbed as the degenerate and unenterprising ghosts of more recent times.'

It is all very strange and mysterious. Why was it necessary for Silky to be so malevolent?

Nottinghamshire: Worksop: Visitation of Poltergeists

Of all supernatural manifestations, poltergeists are the most unpleasant, always on the attack, cruel, merciless in their methods, noisy, persistent and obtrusive. All investigations into this type of ghost seem to end in failure and without even a positive explanation for their behaviour, other than the belief that 'there must be something' when their cases are examined.

One of the most mysterious cases, fully documented by the Society for Psychical Research, concerned the multiple disturbances in a house in Worksop, as first reported in the *Retford and Gainsborough Times* at the beginning of March 1883. Frank Podmore MA has left a detailed report for the Society, whose generous consent has allowed me to give extracts of the result of his investigation at the house of Joe White in Worksop, in order to examine the truth and, if possible, the reason for such inexplicable disturbances. The report is thorough, concise, authentic and as disturbing to read as the case was to Mr Podmore and indeed to the whole town of Worksop, whose inhabitants were convinced there was some trickery about it all.

Mr Podmore arrived on Saturday 7 April 1883 and signed his report on 11 April. Between those dates he examined no fewer than eight principal witnesses, three of them signing depositions; he considered all of them to be reliable and truthful. The eight were Joe White, his brother Tom, 'a bright-looking lad of 18 or 20', Solomon Wass (a neighbour) and his wife, George (Buck) Ford, Police Constable Higgs, Arthur Curras (a coal miner) and Doctor Lloyd.

Joe White had been in residence in his house for three years. The front door was locked and sealed over inside by paper; the house was not very clean and was filled with hung bacon, even the passage, stairs and bedrooms. The first recorded disturbance had appeared on 21 February, when Mrs White was alone with two of the children in the evening; suddenly the table on which she was washing up the tea things tilted alarmingly, the candle went out and she saved the wash-tub from sliding to the floor only by quickly grasping it. Her husband made light of her story when he returned.

White was away for a few days, and his wife allowed a girl, Eliza Rose, to sleep with her. She was the daughter of an imbecile mother and herself not very stable. His brother Tom came back, going upstairs to bed, where the children had gone earlier to sleep. Suddenly Mrs White heard a great noise from the staircase, down which came a corkscrew, clothes pegs and a salt cellar; then a pause before quite incredibly hot coals came bumping down. Tom denied knowing anything about what had happened.

The next night knives, forks, spoons and other articles came hurtling down the stairs, and one of the ornaments on the kitchen shelf leaped across the room and smashed on the floor. The combined screams of Mrs White and Rose brought White downstairs, when he was struck on the forehead by a candle leaving its candlestick. Two more candles were lighted, then a china ornament of a woman flew across the room and back again before the eyes of the so-far dubious White, who was now himself scared; seeing how frightened the women were, he sent for PC Higgs. Since he believed that one of his children, who was ill, might be made worse by these disturbances, he sent for the doctor as well.

All these people then watched as a basin lifted itself from the table, rose to the ceiling, fell down again and smashed to pieces on the floor. Things were becoming serious now that so many people had witnessed inexplicable happenings, with no one but themselves in the house to suspect of trickery.

An additional witness appeared when Arthur Curras, a coal miner and neighbour called at the house. He was '…a very steady, respectable man, a Methodist but very sceptical and believed White did it all but couldn't guess how it was done'. He was called into the house by White himself, as he stated in his deposition:

> I passed by White's house, and hearing a disturbance, I looked over the railings, and White said to me 'There's something in the house that's breaking all afore it.' I asked him what it were, and he told me to come and see …. He took me into the front place where the clock was hanging over the bed's head, and was showing me a nest of drawers, where his suit of clothes came out of the bottom drawer into the top one but one. While I was looking at the drawer, and the broken pots there was lying there, the clock by some means came from the wall, slantingwise about seven feet, and dropped clear of the bed's foot onto the floor. It had been fastened up on the wall, near the bed's head, and it fell between the bed's foot and the door. I said 'What is that?' White said 'It's something else smashed.' I turned round and saw that it was the clock. The nail still remained in the wall. The girl Rose was coming out of the kitchen towards the inner door, but had not got quite up to it. She seemed to be much frightened. White said to me, 'It doesn't matter a damn where that lass goes, there's something smashes.'

The disturbances continued unrelentingly. A Salvation Army woman called to see White. Rose was in the kitchen alone when a candlestick flew from a bin and fell behind the woman, who fled in terror from the house. Ornaments were repeatedly smashed. Everyone became more and more frightened, unable to sleep, no one daring to be alone in any part of the house, until at last White, convinced that Rose was the cause of it all, told her to go. 'After her departure,' reports Mr Podmore, 'nothing whatever of an abnormal character took place, and the house has remained undisturbed up to the present time .... The one motive which I heard suggested – if we disregard a report in one newspaper, subsequently contradicted in another, to the effect that White was anxious to buy the house, and to buy it cheap – was that he produced the disturbances in fulfilment of a sporting bet. But I saw no reason to regard this explanation as anything but a scholium evolved by some ingenious commentator from the facts themselves ... April 11th, 1883.'

More serious poltergeist cases have invariably driven the terrified occupants of the house out of it, even inflicted physical punishment; it is therefore very fortunate that this did not happen to the White family, though the house could never again have meant the same to them. In any case, there is no factual evidence that they did remain there.

Yorkshire: Skipsea: The White Lady of Skipsea Castle

In the history of ghosts there have been numerous white ladies, but surely the most enduring is the beautiful white lady of Skipsea Castle, its isolated ruins standing near the junction of the B1242 and B1249 roads between Bridlington and Hornsea on the east coast. She has made her frantic and hasty appearances for some 900 years, since the Norman Conquest. She has been seen at night and in daylight, a young and beautiful woman with a sad face, dressed in a long white gown. For centuries no local person would go near the castle at night for fear of meeting her as she flitted through the ruins and on the motte, or mound, which still marks what was once her home. She was Aveline, niece of William the Conqueror and wife of Dru or Drogo de Bevere.

Drogo de Bevere was a Flemish mercenary who joined the forces William recruited in Normandy for the invasion of England. He distinguished himself in the battle and as a reward was given the seigniory of the district of Holderness, where he was created the first lord. As a defence against the Danes, who in those times frequently landed at Flamborough for their invasions, Drogo set about building a castle at Skipsea. He assumed a semi-regal authority in the district, which, owing to his peasant upbringing and coarse and brutal manner, became tyrannical, detested by the people whom he considered *his* subjects, not those of King William. His greed and arrogance became intolerable, being severely curbed when he tried to seize Church lands. He was loathed by the Saxons.

King William, quite unaware of what was going on in the seigniory of Holderness and wishing to grant Drogo even more honours, gave him the hand of his niece Aveline in marriage, one of the highest honours any sovereign could bestow. (She was *supposed* to have been one of William's nieces, the granddaughter of William's mother, Herleva, by her second marriage.) Aveline was very beautiful and brought a rich dowry, which automatically became the property of Drogo. After the wedding they resided in the castle Drogo had built.

Almost from the start the marriage was a failure, as was inevitable between a rough and coarse peasant and a cultured Norman lady. The quarrels became more and more bitter, and it did not take long before he was treating her like a serf, as he considered everyone else in the district was. He was also drinking heavily; it was during his bouts that he began to threaten her with death. He became more and more harsh, savage and barbarous, until one night he carried out his threat and poisoned her.

The next day, when Drogo realized the enormity of his murderous act, he was terrified that, when the King found out what he had done, he would be stripped of all his honours and undoubtedly executed for his crime. Without even burying her, he rushed out to his stables and, choosing his best horse, rode as fast as the horse could go, the immense distance to London, with the secret plan he had hastily thought out. When he had been received with favour and joy by William, he outlined his cunning plan. He said that he would like to take his wife to Flanders now that the war was over. He had not seen his native country since the invasion, and it would be a great honour for him to introduce his wife to his parents. As his territory, though vast, was mostly morass and forests, yielding only a few oats, he pleaded he had no money to make his desired journey. William, far from being angry, actually applauded his desire and told him that all the money he needed would be given him from the Treasury; he would command this to be done.

Drogo could not believe in the luck his cunning plan had brought him. Leaving the Court, he went at once to take ship to Flanders, with royal permission to do so. He had scarcely hoisted sail for his journey when messengers arrived from Skipsea with news of the poisoning of Aveline. The infuriated monarch ordered that the first available ship set sail immediately for Flanders. He gave strict orders to pursue and capture Drogo, dead or alive. It was too late, however, for Drogo had had a good start and was, in fact, never seen again.

There is no extant record of what happened to Aveline's body; there was no mention in the Domesday Book of a church in Skipsea, where she would have been buried. It has been stated, however, that Stephen, Earl of Albemarle, to whom William Rufus granted the lordship of the seigniory, '...gave his church of the Castle of Skipsea to the Monastery of Albemarle', so it is probable that this is where her body was laid, the church having been erected after the Domesday survey. Her spirit, though, was earthbound and could never find peace unless and until it found a resting-place. She continued her unhappy and restless haunting even as late as the last century.

The *Hull Advertiser* gave its readers a full account of what must have been the first actual sighting of the phantom of the White Lady, which had previously been only legendary in the rich folklore of Yorkshire. The editor of the paper prefaced the account of the story by saying: 'In introducing the following singular article, it may be necessary to state that the writer as well as the two persons upon whose testimony the circumstances rest, are well known to us, and above all suspicion of having thus related anything save what they believed to be strictly correct.' The article referred to went as follows:

> The writer states that he was visiting a lady in Holderness, when the conversation of the party then assembled turned upon supernatural appearances, the lady expressing the opinion that they 'were owing to some misapprehension of the senses,' upon which a gentleman of the party, of unimpeachable character, said that he was under the necessity of differing from the lady. 'For,' said he, 'about ten years ago I was travelling on horseback one afternoon from Bridlington to Hornsea, and just as I was descending the brow of a hill, on the south of Skipsea, I observed a woman, apparently young, dressed in white, walking a little before me on my left hand, between the hedge and the road. Supposing that she had been visiting a house on the top of the hill, I turned my head to see if there were any persons in attendance at the door, but the door was shut and none to be seen. My curiosity being now greater than before to know who this genteel person was, I followed her at the distance of twenty or thirty yards down the hill, which was 100 or 150 yards long, and expected when she got to the bottom, where there was a small brook, that I should meet her in attempting to gain the carriage bridge, but to my great astonishment, when she approached the brook, instead of turning to the right to gain the bridge, she vanished from my sight, at the very time that my eyes were fixed upon her. As soon as I got home, I related the strange affair to my family; and as it was light, and I had not previously been thinking about apparitions, nor was I ever in the habit of speculating on such subjects, I am firmly persuaded that what I saw was one ....

The lady of the house then told the writer that his account had made a great impression and confirmed what she herself recalled – a similar experience one of her servants had had five years previously. It was in November, at Martinmas, when he had requested permission to go to Bridlington, borrowing a horse for the journey. He set off two hours before daybreak, astonishing her by returning frightened out of his life by what he had seen. His horse had suddenly shied and bolted. Recovering control, he saw a figure all in white standing in the road, a black veil over her head. As he watched, terrified, the figure vanished.

This is the last authentic account of the phantom of the White Lady of Skipsea; perhaps after all the centuries her spirit is, at last, at rest.

The castle was destroyed by soldiers of Henry III.

5   The South East

Hampshire: *Ewshott House: THE Ghost*

Even in the much-haunted countryside surrounding Odiham, Old Basing and Farnham Castle, the fifteenth-century Itchell Manor House, later called Ewshott House, had the reputation of being the most haunted. It stood in the village of Crondall, off the A287 south-east of Odiham. In spite of the variety of its manifestations, in the family papers and accounts one became familiarly referred to by the family merely as 'The Ghost'. The manor was almost totally burned down in the seventeenth century, rebuilt in the eighteenth century and finally demolished in 1954.

The Bathurst family were the owners for over a hundred years, from 1680, and some time during that period a 'Squire' Bathurst was in all probability the origin of 'The Ghost', as distinct from other apparitions. He was a very rich gentleman and a great miser, though he spared nothing on foreign travel. When he was in Italy, he engaged a valet and was so pleased with his service that he brought him back with him to the manor. It was not long after his return that the Squire disappeared, and legend states that he was murdered by his Italian valet for the hoard of treasure in the house. The Italian bricked him up in the walls of one of the many rooms in the house, stole all he could and returned to Italy. It was then that terrifying noises (always at night) earned it the reputation of an evil house in which no one wanted to live.

In the year 1818 the Lefroy family inherited the estate and, well aware they were going to live in a haunted house, moved into it in 1823. They were still there in 1841, if not later, as was evident in an authenticated account by a Captain Frazer RA. In that account, written to his friend Charles Lefroy, he reminds Charles that he was about twelve years old when the family took up residence. It was not long after that the servants began to give notice and leave. Such was the reputation of the house in the village that no locals would replace them.

Even supposing that the Lefroys knew about 'Squire' Bathurst's murder as the cause of 'The Ghost', it would have arisen only from the noises that were in the house, which were beginning to be accepted. They certainly had no idea of the unknown apparition that suddenly appeared whilst a lady of the family was upstairs dressing for a dance in the evening. She heard the sound of horses' hooves and the crunch of wheels on the gravelled drive, indicating that a visitor was calling in a carriage. She listened attentively: the sounds were unmistakable and she waited for someone to ring the bell downstairs. Then, thinking that perhaps no one had heard it, she went downstairs and opened the door. There was no one there, nor any mark on the gravel. Now puzzled and frightened, she ran back upstairs to her room.

She said nothing to anyone about this phantom until later when her fears were corroborated by another person. A young tutor, engaged for the children, was sitting up late one night, in the morning-room, reading and writing in preparation for the next day's work. He was suddenly startled by the crunch of wheels and the hooves of trotting horses on the drive, which ceased when someone had evidently stopped to call, though he felt it must be far too late for a visitor, unless it was a doctor or someone with an urgent message. After a pause he decided to go downstairs but, being new to the house, wandered hopelessly along dark passages and through many rooms. His fears were redoubled, and he was almost in a state of panic when someone, hearing movement, came out, heard the story and led him back to his own room.

When one of the family began investigating this fresh mystery, he discovered that there had been another owner of the manor after the Bathursts had gone and before the Lefroys had arrived. The owner had been driving his coach-and-four across Bagshot Heath when he was halted by a highwayman, demanding his money or his life. Refusing to obey the command to stand and deliver, he attempted to drive on but both he and his postillion were shot dead. The terrified horses bolted, not stopping until they reached the manor, where the wife, hearing the noise, opened the door to find the dead bodies.

It was after the scare of the phantom coach and horses that 'The Ghost' began in real earnest to express itself in terrifying noises night after night, always between midnight and two o'clock. In the daytime, however, Charles Lefroy found that, whenever he came near one of the rooms, called 'the Little Highlander', he always heard hurrying footsteps preceding his approach up the stairs, followed by strange noises in the room, yet whenever he opened the door and went in, there was only silence. He had at first thought it was the room where the 'Squire' was bricked up but he could never be certain.

Guests came and went, servants also; accounts of the noises differed widely; some guests left next day, no longer willing to stay in such a house, but 'The Ghost' continued what were now becoming terrifying ordeals, even for the Lefroys. What made 'The Ghost' unique in the manor, indeed in the whole area, were the pattern and variety of the noises it made. According to Charles Lefroy's friend Captain Frazer (the only authentic authority on the manor and its ghost, at least while he was there): 'The noise generally continued, with intervals, for about two hours; and I think there was a slight interval every *five* blows but am not quite sure about this point.'

At one time the manor had been divided, one half being utilized as a farmhouse. This part had been taken down and removed to a distance from the house itself. During the progress of the work a man had been employed to guard the timber. What he heard in his wanderings around the grounds was unmistakable: noises as if someone was dealing heavy blows with a muffled mallet, night after night 'over against the spot where the old farmhouse was and therefore very near to the place where he watched'.

For some time there had been hostility between the Lefroys and the farmhouse bailiff, each accusing the other of making the noises, and even between guests whose rooms were next to each other. Charles Lefroy himself told

Captain Frazer that one night he had been awakened by a noise on the gravel below his window, 'like a heavily laden cart or carriage carrying a load of iron rods', but when he went to the window there was nothing to be seen. Even more peculiar and conjectural was the report by another guest who was awakened by what seemed to be a flock of sheep rushing by under his window, but he also saw nothing.

Charles Lefroy, by now stupefied, wrote to Captain Frazer, inviting him to come and spend a few days with him in the house – an invitation which the Captain accepted, because, as he said in his letter from Carlisle after he had left the manor, dated 19 July 1841, '...although always much interested in anything partaking of the marvellous I have no faith in superhuman agency. Still it was impossible at night to hear the unaccountable sound without a slight feeling of depression, and I think it would have an [ill] effect upon a person of weak nerves or mind.' His letter is long, sincere, unbiased and authentic as to what happened in the few days he spent in the house haunted by 'The Ghost', where the Lefroys had lived for eighteen years, incredible as it seems that any person could endure such noise for so long and remain sane. There are no details of the date of their departure, and the whole mystery of 'The Ghost' has never been solved; nor is it ever likely to be.

Kent: *Margate: The Haunted Theatre Royal*

Ever since 1874, when the Theatre Royal, Margate, was rebuilt, seating some 2,000 people, under the management of a well-known actress named Sarah Thorne, the theatre has been haunted to such an extent that it has the reputation of being the most haunted theatre in the south of England and even beyond. The sequence of apparitions, noises, slamming of locked doors, switching on and off of electric lights by unseen hands, a Grey Man, a Grey Lady, a suicide and a ball of orange light are but a few of the mysteries. In spite of all these, the dominating spirit and the most often seen was the ghost of Sarah Thorne herself.

The first thing she did was to establish an academy for prospective young actors and actresses who later made their names as Mr and Mrs George Arliss, Mr and Mrs Seymour Hicks and Violet and Irene Vanbrugh, to name only a few, all of them returning to Margate to act in the theatre many times. Dame Irene Vanbrugh, who made her début at the Theatre Royal at the age of fifteen, said of Sarah Thorne: 'She was not a good actress but what a fine teacher she was, though her appearance did not help her, but her ability to teach others was a real gift.'

On 27 February 1899 Sarah died from a severe attack of influenza at her Chatham home; she was sixty-two. Though her home was in Chatham, her heart was in Margate. Her oft-repeated words, used when dying, 'So long as the Theatre Royal is there, I shall be there', were unconsciously prophetic, for her ghost was seen there almost as soon as she had died. Her son told people he had seen his mother many times in the theatre; so too had the Australian manager Caspar Middleton, who knew nothing at all about the hauntings and in any case was not interested in such things. On three separate occasions, however, he had seen the ghost of a woman walking along the back of the circle and disappearing on the other side through a wall, which he later found out was part of Sarah Thorne's office. The second time she appeared so suddenly that he could almost have touched her. The third time she was in the stalls. So clearly had the figure appeared that he later gave an exact description of the dress she wore – as 'bluish-grey draperies flowing and transparent', which he found out to be the stage dress worn by Sarah as Lady Macbeth.

Shortly afterwards, in August, two actresses were rehearsing in the circle buffet when one of them, reading her part, was suddenly alarmed by the sight of someone waving her arms about in one of the boxes. Her screams brought the other actress to her and, terrified at seeing the figure, she collapsed. A third actress was also horrified by the sight of the waving hands and the figure, who wore the clothes Mr Middleton had seen.

There was, however, a far more terrifying theatre ghost than Sarah Thorne's. In the early 1890s one of the actors in a 'stock company', as they were known, travelling all around the country on tour, was dismissed for an unknown reason; angry and embittered by what he thought was gross injustice, 'the Grey Man', as he came to be called, bought a ticket in a stage box for the following night's performance and during one of the acts threw himself from the box into the orchestra pit and broke his neck. Almost immediately his ghost began to appear and with such regularity that alarm spread through the theatre and throughout the town, causing such lack of bookings that the management decided to withdraw the box from use and have the curtains permanently drawn. This had no effect, for ghostly hands would draw the curtains back each time a play began. Finally the box was bricked up, but strange and disturbing noises continued, and no one would go near the box if they could avoid it.

There was one other ghost, known as 'the Grey Lady', not often seen but once witnessed by eight people drinking in the foyer bar, who suddenly saw the figure noiselessly pass from one side of the foyer to another. It was believed to be Sarah Thorne until some years later, when her niece visited the theatre, she said that the Grey Lady was not her aunt but a ghost she had seen soon after she began in the theatre. She had suddenly come face to face with it when going along one of the passages leading to the vault under the theatre. It was all in grey and looked like a nun. She was so terrified that she fainted and was found lying on the floor some three hours later.

The Theatre Royal was closed during World War II, due to damage caused by nearby bombing. It re-opened in the summer of 1948, and the hauntings resumed their possession of it. The theatre was used for repertory performances, then for all-in wrestling, then as a cinema and finally a bingo hall. Sarah Thorne's ghost was not seen during those years. Then, on 23 January 1955, the *Brighton Mail* published a full report on a fresh outbreak of hauntings, which caused widespread interest in the town and even beyond. Lights were switched on when no one was in the theatre to do so, gas heaters were switched on and off, locked doors opened; there were unaccountable noises. Twice the caretaker was called urgently from his home to deal with a police call that the theatre was open and blazing with lights. Accompanied by two members of the Malvern Repertory who were then playing at the theatre, he went to switch off the lights. This done, all the doors were securely locked and the party went home about 1.30. Only forty-five minutes later, the police again called out the caretaker, to find once more the doors unlocked and the lights blazing. For the second time the caretaker switched off the lights and doubly secured the doors, before returning home. He had only been back half an hour when the police called him out for the third time, when the performance was repeated, the constable checking that the outside lock was secure as well as the inside.

A few days later one of the Malvern players, upon leaving the stage door, turned to thank the doorkeeper, only to find there was no one there or in sight. The same experience came when he was entering the same evening, which came as a great shock.

In January 1966, when the theatre was being used as a bingo hall, a painter named Alfred Tanner, working at night, became increasingly mystified by the sound of footsteps and the strange sound of whispering near him, as if between two unseen people. He became alarmed as the sounds increased, especially the footsteps. As they came closer to him, there was a sudden violent bang on one of the doors. He thought it was the box-office door but there was no one there, nor did he hear the footsteps and whispering as he resumed his work. Almost immediately they began again. It was then that a heavy thud echoed through the empty theatre, which might have been the sound of the Grey Man throwing himself from the stage box. Though Tanner saw nothing but dust rising from the stage, it did not deter him. The next night he resumed his painting when suddenly he really was frightened by the sight of the ball of orange light, which he had not even heard of. It passed rapidly across the stage within inches of his face and vanished through the Exit door to the street.

In 1972, again in January, the ball of orange light was seen by another painter. No satisfactory reason for such a phenomenon has ever been offered.

In that same year the *Isle of Thanet Gazette* reported that Mother Olandah, a clairvoyant who had worked closely with Gypsy Lee before his death, had been called in to investigate the hauntings. She corroborated that the vision she had of Sarah Thorne was a very real one, and she had no doubt whatsoever that it was she. The dress she wore '…was a lovely crinoline in pastel shades with a leaf and floral design'. The actress had given her a message, complaining about '…the leaf on my dress. Oh, the poor leaf.' Mother Olandah was told that previously a painter had covered part of a gold-leaf wallpaper with brown paint.

The last sighting of Sarah Thorne was in 1972, and again by a painter working one night in the bingo hall, which recalls the actress's own words on her deathbed: 'As long as there is a Theatre Royal, I shall be there.'

Kent: Wrotham: The Man in Grey

In the spring of 1880 Captain and Mrs Brooke received an invitation to take their child for a week's holiday at Wrotham House in Wrotham, some eight miles from Maidstone. The Captain, whose regiment was stationed at Chatham nearby, was unable to accept, but he urged his wife to do so, as their daughter had not been well and the change would be beneficial for her. At first Mrs Brooke demurred, reminding her husband of the bad time they had had there in the autumn of the previous year, when they had been unable to sleep because of the icy-cold rooms, and their determination never to return there. It had been an unforgettable cold, and had either of them had the slightest idea of the supernatural, they would not only have understood the cause of it but certainly never have considered returning there. However, Mrs Brooke decided to give the place another chance, as it was springtime and very much warmer, though before her complete acceptance of the invitation, she requested rooms that were warmer. Then, together with her child and nurse, she set out for the rambling old historic house with some degree of anxiety.

Her anxiety was fully justified when they arrived on the Saturday to find that their hostess, totally ignoring her guest's request, with an astonishing lack of courtesy and hospitality, had given them the same rooms. They consisted of a very large bedroom and a dressing-room a few yards along the passage in the farthest wing of the house. Mrs Brooke, saying nothing but thinking much, could do little except to ask the nurse to sleep in the dressing-room whilst she and the child would sleep in the big bedroom. She had no sooner opened the door than the cold struck her as much as it had before, in spite of the much warmer weather. This filled her with a premonition of something quite unknown to her, and she was already regretting her acceptance of the invitation.

After dinner that evening she sat up late talking to her hostess. She remembered later that, as she passed through the hall to go to bed, she had heard a grandfather clock striking midnight. When she now opened the door of her room, intense cold completely enveloped her. She went anxiously to the bed, where she found her daughter sleeping soundly. After undressing and slipping into bed beside the child, she began shivering with cold, although the child was warm.

On Sunday morning at eight o'clock the nurse came in. Her face was white, more with fear than cold; her eyes were red and her hands trembling. When her mistress asked her if she was ill, as she looked so unwell, she said:

'As the clock was striking one someone must have been playing practical jokes on me because I heard footsteps up and down the passage for some time, before they stopped outside my door and it suddenly opened.'

'Why didn't you lock your door?' asked Mrs Brooke.

'I did lock it. Twice. But it opened again. I was terrified.'

Mrs Brooke tried to cheer her, teasing her with eating too much supper and telling her to go down to breakfast before she herself did so. After breakfast the nurse returned, this time with an excited look in her eyes as she said, 'Oh, ma'am, is it not too bad? The servants have told me the rooms are haunted, and the doors must never be closed until after one o'clock.'

Mrs Brooke told her she would make her own enquiries from their hostess but in the meantime she was not to worry.

After returning from church with her hostess, Mrs Brooke began asking about the house generally. How old was it? Who had lived there? Was the room in which she was sleeping haunted? At the last word she noticed a swift exchange of meaningful glances between her hostess and her daughter. After a pause the daughter said, 'Yes, there is a haunted room but we will not tell you where it is as you might begin to imagine things.'

'I think I know the room already, and my nurse was frightened by the ghost last night.'

Mother and daughter declined to say any more, other than to offer to have one of the under-servants sleep with the nurse if she would like it. Mrs Brooke agreed to that, so the nurse and the under-servant occupied the dressing-room for the night, while Mrs Brooke, strangely less afraid than curious, decided it would be sensible not only to lock her door securely but to prop a chair under the door-handle as well. She then undressed and got into bed. The intense cold was both in the room and in the bed, though once again the child seemed not to have been disturbed by anything. The cold increased, and she knew she could only lie and wait, for to sleep was impossible.

It was not long before she heard footsteps in the passage, passing her door and back again, then suddenly halting outside and pausing; then began a fumbling at the door-handle. She was now seriously alarmed and even began to pray for help of some kind as the door, quite soundlessly, began to open, in spite of the chair propped under the handle.

Suddenly there was a pale light in the room, quite distinct from the flickering fire-light. The figure of a man, walking very deliberately, moved towards the foot of the bed. He was dressed in a grey suit trimmed with silver and wearing a cocked hat, and his face was turned away from the window.

Mrs Brooke lay in terror watching him. His back was towards her, so that she could not see his face as he stood there, before going out of the room, along the passage, up and down for a while and then again returning. Finally he went out for the last time, uttering a diabolical laugh as he went, leaving Mrs Brooke motionless with abject terror. The clock struck two and she must have slept, for the next sound was the servant knocking on the door, pushing it open and moving the chair.

Mrs Brooke said nothing at all to her hostess but decided that the nurse should sleep in the bedroom with her and the child, as double security and a witness to whatever might happen. The nurse agreed willingly. After settling the child to sleep, Mrs Brooke went down to dinner, leaving the nurse to follow when the child was asleep. They were both very tired, and Mrs Brooke decided to go to bed early and get some sleep. It was about half past ten when they settled down in the beds. In spite of the fire, Mrs Brooke still felt intensely cold, as did the nurse. Mrs Brooke lighted a candle and after double-locking the door undressed and crept into an ice-cold bed next to her daughter, who was warm and breathing quietly.

She awoke as midnight was striking and whispered to the nurse to see if she was asleep, only to hear her whisper back: 'I hear steps, ma'am. Do you?'

'Yes,' she said. 'I will get up and meet whatever it is.'

She tried to rise but was quite unable to move and felt as if she were being held down. Any courage she had left disappeared as the door noiselessly opened. Once again she watched in terror as the man in grey entered the room and moved with slow deliberation to the end of her bed, his back towards her, facing the window for a long time. Then, as he gave a laugh that chilled her spine, Mrs Brooke watched the ghost go out of the room. Only then did she move and whisper to the nurse, who informed her that she, too, had seen the ghost and heard its maniacal laugh as it retreated along the passage.

'Tomorrow we leave! Not another night here!' said Mrs Brooke.

At breakfast in the morning she told her hostess and her

daughter what she and the nurse had seen and heard and that they could not spend another night in the house. Both protested, assuring her that the ghost would not return, that he appeared only three times and always only to strangers, that he would never harm then. Mrs Brooke categorically refused to stay and said they would depart as soon as they had packed their things.

'In doing so,' continued Mrs Brooke when recording her experiences, 'I knew I was forfeiting our friendship. I believe the family has suffered from these visitations for seventy-five years, and that the ghost is supposed to be that of a man who murdered his brother in the room in which I slept, and threw the body out of the window. I am told that there is in existence a portrait of one of these brothers, dressed as I have described him.'

This authentic ghost story was told by Mrs Brooke to the Bishop of Hyères in the south of France, adding that corroboration of her story could be obtained from the nurse, Mrs Page. The nurse wrote a letter confirming every detail of her mistress's account of the apparition which she herself had also witnessed. The two documents, dated 29 April 1883, were sent to Lord Halifax, who published the facts in his *Ghost Book*, first published in 1936. It was rightly considered by his son, the Earl of Halifax KG to be one of the most celebrated collections of ghost stories in the English language, as he stated in the preface to his father's book.

Sussex: Hurstmonceux: The Drummer Ghost

The magnificent moated castle of Hurstmonceux was named after the Norman lord Waleran de Monceux. From an heiress of this family the manor passed to the Fiennes family and to Sir Richard Fiennes, who became Lord Dacre of the South. The family retained it until 1708, since when it has passed through many hands; from 1948, however, it has housed the Royal Observatory, driven out of Greenwich by pollution interfering with astronomy.

Throughout the centuries the castle has been haunted by a variety of ghosts and not surprisingly by a Phantom Drummer who occupied a room in the entrance tower of the castle called 'the Drummer's Hall'. He guarded the treasure there, and the tattoo of his drum could often be heard at and after midnight. He was supposed to have been personal trumpeter to Sir John Fiennes at the battle of Agincourt, where he was killed on St Crispin's Day 1415. Such was his devotion and loyalty to his master that legend says his shade accompanied him after the victorious battle, returning with him to his castle. Addison wrote a play about it, and Baxter recorded it in his book *The Invisible World*.

'The unearthly drum of Hurstmonceux', however, was said to have had a more sinister meaning – invented by one of the Lords Dacre who employed a French gardener to beat a drum at night when smugglers were bringing contraband to the castle during his absence. This was to avoid suspicion as to what was going on while the fine French brandy was filling his cellars. Another Lord Dacre, an elderly man, seems to have had far more interesting reasons for beating drum tattoos. He decided to become an anchorite and built himself a hermitage in a part of his estate, where he lived on bread and water and prayers. Since he had abandoned his young and gay wife for no satisfactory reason, and determined to keep any over-adventurous men from pursuing her, he beat warning tattoos on the drum he kept hidden in the hermitage. His resentful wife, however, decided she had had enough, so she ordered that his cell be sealed up and left him to die of starvation.

There were other ghosts to take the place of the Phantom Drummer. One was of a man with a pigtail, dressed as a sailor, who might easily have been associated with the smugglers and the drum-beating French gardener. In the year 1727 a new apparition appeared, wandering among the ruins of parts of the castle. She was believed to have been an heiress who had been starved to death in one of the castle rooms by her governess, who had been bribed to do this by another member of the family, to prevent the heiress from inheriting the property.

Of all these ghosts, however, the most authentic seem to be those of the hunting party of men moving about at night. There were four of them, all dressed in the clothes worn during the reign of Henry VIII. They were the ninth Baron Dacre of the South and his three cronies, George Roydon, John Mantell and Frowdys. Lord Dacre, a wild and irresponsible man, suggested to his boon companions that they should wait until a moonlight night and go out together to kill a deer on the adjoining estate of Sir Nicholas Pelham. The joke was eagerly welcomed by the reckless quartet, who set out a few nights later. They rode swiftly and silently across the fields dividing the two estates.

As they reached the Cuckmere river, they were spotted and challenged by Sir Nicholas' gamekeeper and two companions, being ordered off the land, a demand met with jeering laughter. The gamekeepr at once attacked them with his staff, assisted by his two colleagues, at which Lord Dacre's party drew their swords. The woods echoed with the clash of swords and noise of staves striking trees, until, with a cry, the gamekeeper fell to the ground, blood spurting from a sword wound. In panic Lord Dacre's men galloped off as fast as their horses could move, the wounded gamekeeper being carried away by his two companions.

When Sir Nicholas Pelham was awakened with the news of what had happened, the gamekeeper was able to tell him that he had identified Lord Dacre as one of the party, a statement confirmed by his two assistants. The gamekeeper died two days later, and Sir Nicholas had Lord Dacre and his cronies charged with murder, corroborated by the two witnesses. When the news of this came to public notice, disputes arose, as some people considered the charge should have been one of manslaughter rather than murder. All four were arrested and imprisoned. Because Lord Dacre was a peer, he was entitled to be tried by peers, who would pass sentence. He, therefore, was imprisoned in the Tower of London. Sentence of death was passed on all four.

There, was however, just a chance that Henry VIII himself might take the view that, because Lord Dacre 'was in another part of the wood in the affray', he would receive a reprieve. The great chronicler Holinshed wrote: 'On the 18th June the sheriffs of London were ready in the Tower to receive the prisoner and lead him to execution on Tower Hill; but a gentleman of the Lord Chancellor's house came and in the King's name commanded to stay execution till two in the afternoon, which caused many to think that the King would have granted him his pardon.' As there was no further word from the king, the four prisoners were taken in a cart to Tyburn, where they were all hanged. It was said that the Phantom Drummer beat a tattoo in the Drummer's Room as they mounted the scaffold.

Sussex: Midhurst – Cowdray House: The Cowdray Curse

One of the worst forms of haunting in ghost history is the curse. This is perhaps because it is not visible as an apparition, and the effects are, therefore, even more disturbing and frightening since it is constant. There have not been a great number of recorded curses, but those which have been recorded are concentrated on castles, abbeys and great houses, and always upon the families who have lived there for a very long time, even centuries. Cowdray House must be unique, since the ancient and distinguished family of the Brownes, later created Viscounts Montague, who lived there for nearly four centuries, had not one but two curses put upon it.

There are few more romantic and picturesque ruins in the British Isles than Cowdray House, reached by a causeway running across the meadows from the main street of Midhurst. Nearly two centuries have passed since it was completely gutted by fire; charred remains can still be seen of its splendid Great Parlour, Great Hall and Chapel. It was built by Sir William Fitzwilliam (later Earl of Southampton) in the years 1532-3 on the site of the manor of Cowdray. In 1536, when Henry VIII dissolved the monasteries and religious houses, the king granted Sir William all the adjacent lands and the thirteenth-century Priory of Easebourne in Midhurst, from which the nuns were to be ejected, by force if necessary, and their goods and treasures confiscated.

Legend has it that the first curse, the Curse of Heaven, was put upon both house and family by the Sub-Prioress before she was driven out. It is said she called on Heaven that the curse should continue until the male line of the owners should become extinct.

In 1538, King Henry VIII dissolved the rich and powerful Abbey of Hastings with all its lands, granting it to Sir Anthony Browne, Master of Horse to the king and Standard Bearer of England. He was Sir William Fitzwilliam's half-brother, both of whom were held in high esteem. A second legend gives a far more detailed account of the second curse. It is said that the arrogance and conduct of Sir Anthony disgusted and shamed the monks, both by his attitude towards them and their beloved Abbey and his 'high revelry' in a religious house. The crisis came one night, when at a banquet held by Sir Anthony in the refectory, he sent for the Abbot and ordered both him and all his Benedictine monks to leave the Abbey for ever. The announcement was made from the High Table, as shouts and laughter broke out from the many drunken guests. Suddenly there was a great silence as the Abbot pointed his finger at Sir Anthony and uttered his terrible curse. He cursed them 'in sleeping and waking, in eating and drinking, in all their incomings and outgoings, until fire and water should destroy their house and extinguish their family and all their posterity for ever.' Then still in silence he turned and left the hall and the Abbey.

Ten years later Sir Anthony died; his son, also Sir Anthony went to live in Cowdray House, already cursed by Heaven, a fact of which he undoubtedly had been informed by Lord Southampton before he died in 1542. Sir

Anthony, like his father and indeed all his descendants, was a devoted Roman Catholic and he was created the first Viscount Montague by 'Bloody' Queen Mary; although a Catholic, he was highly esteemed by Queen Elizabeth during his lifetime and was honoured by her historic visit to Cowdray House.

His son, the second Viscount was the first to be reminded by the curse that misfortune lay ahead, for he was involved in the Gunpowder Plot during the reign of James I, only escaping execution by paying a heavy fine and suffering imprisonment in the Tower. Francis Browne, third Viscount, suffered heavily as a Royalist during the Civil Wars, all his estates, including Battle Abbey were sequestrated by the Commonwealth and all his plate and silver was confiscated. Cowdray House was garrisoned by the Roundheads until the Restoration, narrowly escaping complete destruction. Henry, fifth Viscount, a man of uncontrollable outbursts of violent temper, was said to have murdered his priest because he began Mass before his master had entered the chapel.

Through the years the curses can never have been forgotten by the successive owners of Cowdray House. They were like a smouldering and always threatening volcano, which suddenly erupted and burst upon the eighth Viscount, George Samuel, in his twenty-fifth year, exacting a tragic and terrible penalty in revenge by the monks and nuns for being dismissed from their homes. In the summer of 1793, that most fateful and disastrous year in the history of the Montagues of Cowdray, the Viscount left for Switzerland with a friend to shoot the dangerous Schaffhausen rapids in a flat-bottomed boat, evading the magistrate's instructions to the police to prevent them. They succeeded in successfully shooting the first fall, but disaster struck them at the second fall, and both were drowned at Laufenburg, where the Viscount was buried. The estates, but not the title passed to his sister Elizabeth Mary.

After the accident, the Swiss police at once sent a messenger to inform the Viscount's sister of the tragic news. She had married William Stephen Poyntz (of that ancient and illustrious family). They had already despatched a messenger to recall the Viscount, telling him that an accidental fire had completely gutted Cowdray House and its contents. Incredible as it may seem, the messengers met at Calais.

Yet there was still more vengeance to come, for the Abbot of Battle Abbey had included posterity in his curse. Some seventeen years later the Poyntz family decided to go to Bognor for a holiday. In spite of Mrs Poyntz's warnings that the curses might even mean them, her husband laughed at her fears. She pleaded even more with him when he suggested taking their two sons out to sea in a boat. It was a beautiful summer day and the sea was calm. Within a short time, black clouds began to gather and a sudden storm broke out which overturned the boat; the two boys were drowned and their father and the boatman forced to swim for their lives to reach the shore. Mrs Poyntz, who had witnessed the tragedy from the window of the house, never recovered from the shock and died five years later in 1815. She was buried with her two sons in the family vault in Easebourne church.

Mr Poyntz, before his own death from a hunting accident some years later, had completed the rebuilding of the nuns' church where the Curse of Heaven had been uttered by the Sub-Prioress three centuries earlier. It was dedicated as a memorial chapel to the Browne and Poyntz families, who had paid so high a price. Perhaps, thereby, he hoped to bring peace to all concerned in the double curse.

The Cowdray estates were bought by Sir Weetman Dickinson Pearson, Bt., later created first Viscount Cowdray. It was he who carried out the splendid restoration of the ruins of Cowdray House standing today.

6 The South West

Avon: Bristol: The Black Monk of the Vicarage

In 1539, three years after Henry VIII dissolved the monasteries, he ordered all the rich churches to give up their plate and treasures. One of these was All Saints, on the corner of Corn Street and High Street in Bristol, which was considered to be a West Country treasure-house. The then priest gave orders to hide the wealth of silver, gold and jewels in any place that was secret and safe.

Adjoining the church was a building which was the residence of the ancient Guild of Calendarers, who arranged, analysed and indexed ancient and precious documents. Henry also dissolved them and took away their valuable documents. The suspicious and greedy King, despite the plunder he had taken away, was still convinced there was more, so a second search was made, to be sure the place had been thoroughly ransacked.

Almost three centuries passed before any evidence was produced to corroborate strange and mysterious rumours beginning to circulate that the vicarage of All Saints was haunted. In 1846 the *Bristol Times* published an article headed 'A Ghost at Bristol'. The style was slightly derisive and sarcastic, beginning with the words: 'We have this week a ghost story to relate. Yes, a real ghost story and a ghost story without as yet any clue to its elucidation.' At that time the ancient residence of the Guild of Calendarers had been converted into a vicarage-house, called so by the many incumbents who had long ceased to reside there. It was then occupied by Mr and Mrs Jones, the sexton of the church and his wife, one or two lodgers and the servant-maid, who separately and jointly had begun to hear strange and inexplicable noises; worse still, there had been nightly visitations by a black monk that caused much terror to the inhabitants. The visitor could be heard walking about the house. Mr Jones was by no means a nervous man but became alarmed when he began to see flickering lights on the walls. His wife was equally frightened by the nightly noise of creaking shoes, worn by a man wandering up and down the bedroom above her own, '...where no man was on the premises', she told the *Bristol Times*, 'or ought not to be'. The reporter added that, 'She was nearly killed with the fright.'

It was the servant-maid who had the worst shock, when she saw the apparition push open her locked bedroom door one night. She had repeatedly had her bedroom door unbolted at night between the hours of midnight and two o'clock and had covered her head with the bed quilt, too terrified to see the night prowler. But one night she saw him by accident and told the reporter: 'It was wearing something antique "lang syne gune". It was a whiskered gentleman who had gone to the length of shaking her bed and would have shaken her also, she believed.' The reporter added to his account her comment, '...that it caused excessive trembling and the complete doubling up of her whole body into a round ball like'.

When the story came to the ears of Mrs Crowe, author of *The Night Side of Nature*, 1848, she wrote to the *Bristol Times* to ask if there had ever been a solution to the problem. Their reply was as follows: 'The whole affair is wrapped in the same mystery as when chronicled in the pages of the paper, subsequently confirmed by Mrs Jones.'

There were, however, other later occupants of the house who endured the same scares and anxieties that Mrs Jones had seen and heard. A black monk was described as the night prowler who beckoned to them to follow him through a bricked-up wall and then vanished. Was he perhaps one of those who had secreted the considerable treasures of the church at the time of its dissolution? One can only continue to speculate.

The White Lady

In the year 1854 a Mrs Harford lived in a large, rambling fourteenth-century house near Bristol called Stapleton Manor House. The date had been found carved on an old oak beam by workmen doing repairs in the roof. The two bedrooms below were wainscoted and gave out hollow sounds whenever struck by anything heavy, quite possibly used as secret hiding-places if the panels were removed, which no one had ever attempted to do. Mrs Harford was quite aware that the house had the reputation of being haunted; it had lowered the price she paid for it, and she was not unduly frightened of the supernatural. Strange noises there certainly were in odd parts of the house, and guests and staff had seen flickering lights, but no one seemed to be scared.

Mrs Harford's bedroom was on the third floor, a large room with bow windows, containing two beds. She and her invalid sister occupied the large bed, and their other sister the smaller one. A night-light was always kept burning. Being awakened one night by an unusual noise, Mrs Harford saw to her astonishment a white female figure pass slowly across the foot of the bed, moving towards the windows. It moved with purposeful deliberation before her eyes, a slight figure with a fair, sad face, dressed in a white nightcap and a white nightdress. It was so like her sister in the bed that she thought it was she who had got up because she was feeling ill. Not speaking to her sister, because she knew she had a great dislike of being watched at any time by anyone, she turned stealthily round to see if the bed were empty, only to see her sister lying there, peacefully sleeping. Her other sister was also quietly sleeping.

Creeping out of bed, Mrs Harford examined every corner of the room. The windows were fastened; the door was double-bolted; this room was papered not panelled, so there was no possibility of anyone entering or hiding in the room. She mentioned her experience the next day, but no one else had seen or heard anything.

Curiously, some years passed before the figure

appeared again to Mrs Harford, this time standing by her bed and gazing down at her. She was at the time alone in the room and, starting up with terror, saw the figure vanish.

To her astonishment, when she spoke to a new servant who had arrived only a few days before, she told her she also had seen the figure – at five o'clock in the morning when she arose to do her housework. It was the same time as her mistress had seen the apparition. Both room doors had been bolted. The servant had watched the white figure pass through her bedroom door and heard it moving quietly along the passage to her mistress's room. When the housekeeper heard the servant telling the story, she tried to persuade her that it must have been one of the other servants, fearing that the experience would cause her to leave. Although the servant stayed on, she persisted in her statement that it was not another servant at all, for she had seen the fair white face of the figure, which did not resemble anyone in the house.

Years passed but nothing more was ever heard about noises, and no one ever again saw the mysterious white lady in the nightcap and nightdress.

Cornwall: Dozmary Pool: The Evil Spirit of Tregeagle

The haunted Dozmary Pool is in the parish of Bolventor, on the A30 road across Bodmin Moor, the turning to the pool being opposite Jamaica Inn, made famous by Daphne du Maurier in her novel of that name. Cornish legend has long established that it was into this pool that the dying King Arthur commanded his faithful knight Sir Bedevere to throw his precious sword Excalibur, seized by a thrice-waving hand before it disappeared. He had lost his last battle against Mordred at Slaughter Bridge on the River Camel. Though the north-east part of Cornwall in particular is haunted by King Arthur, the haunting of Dozmary Pool is dominated by the evil spirit of the cruel and ruthless magistrate Tregeagle. Even today, 'to roar like Tregeagle' is a time-honoured saying in Cornwall.

Dozmary Pool is unique in Cornwall, and probably in England, for it is a fresh-water lake a thousand feet above sea-level, over a mile in circumference; no hills tower over it, and for centuries it was believed to be bottomless and not fed by any streams, though these theories have been scientifically disproved. It has, however, never lost its sinister, even frightening feeling, especially when storms rage across the treacherous Bodmin Moor with full Atlantic ferocity. It is a dangerous pool, with many moods, sinister and disturbing even on a windless day, when the surface has an immovable, frozen appearance; ominous when the water is ruffled; menacing when high winds blow, totally belying that it is actually only five feet deep, closed in by peat and heather and the limitless space of the moors. It is a danger even today to unwary travellers because of its marshes, hidden streams and bogs. It has all been brilliantly and eerily described by Daphne du Maurier.

Tregeagle haunts not only Dozmary Pool but much of the moor, the rocky Cornish coasts, coves and sand dunes, the church of St Breock, where he was buried, Padstow and Land's End, and is an integral part of the legends and folklore of Cornwall. The whole story of Tregeagle is mythological, resembling as it does the story of Faust and Mephistopheles, for the Devil and the Church contended for his spirit too.

The most popular story states that Tregeagle was a rich and powerful man, guilty of murder, incest and other heinous crimes, living near Dozmary Pool, and that after his death his spirit haunted the area until it was exorcised and laid to rest in the pool. He was not only a rapacious and cruel landlord whom all his tenants feared but also a tyrannical magistrate, and his wife and children were victims of his cruelty. His death came as an immense relief to the whole of Cornwall, for his notorious conduct had reached all parts.

It was said that the Devil waited to secure his soul and

that Tregeagle, terrified by its power, gave a considerable part of his wealth to a nearby monastery in return for monks' promises of ceaseless prayer for, and salvation of, his soul. On his death he was buried with high honours by monks in the church of St Breock, their monastery now enriched by his wealth. They sang psalms and said prayers above his grave to make sure they would retain the custody of his soul. The Devil, however, had other powers, and open war began between Satan and God.

A dispute arose after Tregeagle's death between two tenants, both wealthy, respecting extensive lands they held around Bodmin. Tregeagle had been steward to one of the tenants and had forged deeds, destroyed others, falsified documents and caused chaos by claiming to be the real owner. He had sold large portions of the land, and other parts were leased on long terms, he having received and appropriated all the money. Lawyers fought tenaciously for their respective clients, but the trials had been deferred again and again by the Justices of the Assizes until they finally decided that a day of settlement must be made and judgment given. Witnesses were numerous on both sides, but the day eventually came when the judge decided he could begin his summing-up.

At that exact moment there were sounds of disturbance in the outer building. An intense cold and terrifying silence descended as a defendant entered together with another witness who, he told the judge, had not been previously called. In complete silence the assembled court watched as the spectre of Tregeagle himself stepped into the witness box for his examination by a trembling and white-faced prosecuting counsel.

The awestruck judge, lawyers, witnesses and jury heard, as the spectre stood in silence, the whole system of frauds perpetrated against the defendant. Eventually, after the summing-up by the judge, the jury retired and returned with a verdict: 'guilty' on all charges.

The trial over, everyone expected the spectre to be removed and taken down to the cells. There he stood, powerless to move, although his desire to do so was evident. 'There was a struggle between the angels of darkness and of light for this sinner's soul,' says the legend.

At length the judge, with dignity, commanded that the witness be removed. 'To bring him from the grave has been for me so dreadful a task that I leave him to your care and that of the priors by whom he was so beloved,' was the reply of the defendant. He then left the court. The churchmen were called in, and long disputations began between them and the lawyers as to Tregeagle's punishment for his crimes. The result of hours of argument was that for mitigation of punishment the accused must perform some task so difficult as to be beyond human nature, and thus satisfy the angels on both sides. All agreed. This punishment could be extended into eternity but it would give the accused time to repent all his evil and cruel deeds. Labour must be restless and forever, to prevent the angels of death having victory over the Church, otherwise his fate would be much worse.

The tasks were then chosen:

> One of the lawyers, remembering that Dozmary Pool was bottomless, proposed that Tregeagle might be employed to empty this profound lake. Then one of the churchmen proposed that to make the task more difficult Tregeagle should fulfil this task with a limpet shell having a hole in it .... This was agreed. The spectre of Tregeagle was then removed, carried to Bodmin Moor and set to work. There day after day, week after week, month after month, year after year, storm and shine Tregeagle bent over the dark water working hard with his perforated shell, yet the Pool continued to keep the same level.

In fury, the Devil sent storms, gales, snow and ice to prevent Tregeagle's carrying out his work. In his *Popular Romances of the West of England*, Robert Hunt FRS has given a graphic series of excerpts about all the subsequent tasks Tregeagle was set in the area:

> Lightnings flashed and coiled like fiery snakes around the rocks of Roughtor. Fireballs fell on the desert moors and hissed in the accursed lake. Thunders appealed from the heavens and echoed from hill to hill, an earthquake shook the solid earth and terror was on all living. The winds arose and raged with a fury that was irresistible and hail beat so mercilessly on all things that it spread death around. Long

did Tregeagle stand the pelting of the pitiless storm but at length he yielded to its force and fled. The Demons in crowds were at his heels. He doubled, however, on his pursuers and returned to the lake, but so rapid were they that he could not rest for the required moments to dip his shell in the now seething waters. Three times he fled round the lake and the Evil Ones pursued him, then feeling that there was no safety for him near Dozmary Pool he sprang swifter than the wind across it, shrieking with agony and thus since the Devils cannot cross water and were obliged to go round the lake he gained on them and fled over the moor. The inhabitants of the moor and the neighbouring towns slept not a wink that night .... Even until today is Tregeagle labouring at his task. In calms his wailings are heard; and those sounds which some call the 'soughing of the wind' are known to be the moanings of Tregeagle; while the coming storms are predicted by the fearful roarings of the condemned mortal.

Surely the greatest challenge to any disbeliever in the supernatural would be to find himself or herself lost on Bodmin Moor near Dozmary Pool in a howling Atlantic gale and not have any fear.

Cornwall: Wadebridge and Bodmin Moor: The Double Murders

No parts of Cornwall, surely, are more haunted than Egloshayle in the Wadebridge valley and nearby grim and lonely Bodmin Moor. These places have been the scene of two of the most gruesome murders, which have become a part of Cornish legend and folklore.

The first case has produced an authentic account of one of the most remarkable warning-dreams in ghost history. In the churchyard of the church in Egloshayle, near the road, is the gravestone of Nevell Norway, who was brutally murdered on 8 February 1840. He was the ancestor of Arthur Norway, author of *Highways and Byways of Cornwall,* and of the popular novelist Neville Norway Shute.

The Cornish gentleman Mr Nevell Norway was returning home in the evening on horseback from Bodmin market to his house in Wadebridge when he was attacked by two men lying in wait for him, who obviously knew his movements. His assailants were the brothers James and William Lightfoot. It was a brutal murder, and particularly so because his body was actually transported to the brothers' cottage in Nanstallon, although another version states that they flung the body into a stream, after robbing it, where it was discovered by one of Mr Norway's servants, who had searched the road all through the night after his master had not returned.

The murder might not stand out from any other murder, since all are brutal, by whatever means. Its outstanding interest is the evidence of its entry into the supernatural world, hundreds of miles away, as recorded by Dr Clement Carlyon in his *Early Years and Late Reflections.* 'At that time,' he writes, 'his brother Mr Edmund Norway was in command of a merchant vessel, the *Orient,* on her voyage from Manilla to Cadiz; and the following is his own account of a dream which he had on the night when his brother was murdered.'

> Ship *Orient* from Manilla to Cadiz
> February 8, 1840.

About 7.30 p.m., the island of St. Helena N.N.W., distant about seven miles; shortened sail and rounded to with the ship's head to the eastward; at eight, set the watch and went below; wrote a letter to my brother, Nevell Norway. About twenty minutes or a quarter before ten o'clock, went to bed; fell asleep, and dreamt I saw two men attack my brother and murder him. One caught the horse by the bridle, and snapped a pistol twice, but I heard no report; he then struck him a blow, and he fell off the horse. They struck him several blows, and dragged him by the shoulders across the road and left him. In my dream, there was a house on the left-hand side of the road. At four o'clock I was called, and went on deck to take charge of the ship. I told the second officer, Mr Henry Wren, that I had

had a dreadful dream – namely, that my brother Nevell, was murdered by two men on the road from St. Columb to Wadebridge, but that I felt sure it could not be there, as the house there would be on the right-hand side of the road; so that it must have been somewhere else. He replied: 'Don't think anything about it; you west-country people are so superstitious. You will make yourself miserable the remainder of the voyage.' He then left the general orders and went below. It was one continued dream, from the time I fell asleep until I was called, at four o'clock in the morning.

Edmund Norway,
Chief Officer, ship *Orient*.

This ends the captain's account of his dream, quoted in Dr Carlyon's book. It is interesting to note that in the confession of one of the murderers the details of the dream are fully corroborated.

Only four years later another murder took place, this time on Bodmin Moor. It is still one of the loneliest places in Cornwall, not a place to be on at night, in fog or during bad weather, for one can feel the eeriness of it and believe in hauntings, especially in old ruined farmhouses. Such a one began in the year 1844, when Charlotte Dymond, an attractive girl of eighteen, lost her life by being murdered.

She helped a widow, Mrs Philippa Peter, in Lower Penhale farm in the parish of Davidstow. It was a hard life, for the land was poor, and peat-cutting was not easy. The widow also had help from her son John, a servant John Stevens and a lame labourer called Matthew Weeks, together with Charlotte, who was the milkmaid. In the winter there was nowhere to go and nothing to do except if it was fine, to go to chapel, which was two miles away in the hamlet of Tremail. All was well until Matthew began taking more than a casual interest in Charlotte, which disturbed Mrs Peter, for he began to show his jealousy of her with anyone else. Charlotte herself was not adverse to his attentions, and indeed there were few opportunities for flirtations elsewhere. This did not stop her pretending to Matthew that there were other boys after her, little knowing she was fanning the flames of his jealousy, particularly of one Tommy Prout.

On a lovely spring morning in April 1844, dressed in her best 'courting clothes', she went for what was to be her last walk with Matthew. Unknown to her, he had a knife in his pocket and murder in his heart. In a brutal outburst of jealous anger, he cut her throat from ear to ear. Her body was found in a very lonely spot near Roughtor by a constable.

Matthew attempted to escape but was caught on Plymouth Hoe. He was tried at Bodmin on 9 August and hanged three days later. The executioner was George Mitchell, who had also executed the murderers of Nevell Norway. For some inexplicable reason, according to the account for the Lent Assize at Bodmin, '...he was not allowed his salary until the summer Assize when he was paid £26 for executing Matthew Weeks for murdering Charlotte Dymond.'

At the foot of Roughtor, by the stream where Charlotte's body was found, a stone monument was erected. It reads:

> Monument erected by private subscription in memory of Charlotte Dymond who was murdered by Matthew Weeks, Sunday April 14th, 1844.

The whole area is haunted, as are the graveyard and the place where Nevell Norway was murdered, which seems to indicate a strange bond between two perfectly innocent people living only a few miles apart, perhaps known to each other only in death.

Within the past hundred years, the ghost of Charlotte was plainly seen by a stranger to Cornwall who knew nothing of her murder. He had been fishing all day in the streams of Bodmin Moor and was going home towards evening when he suddenly saw the figure of a young girl on the marshes near a little stream which he had to cross. She was dressed in a coloured gown, wearing a red shawl and a silk bonnet. She was walking carefully, her eyes gazing down on the marshy ground. As she passed him, he called out 'Good night', but she made no answer. She kept stopping and staring across the moor as if searching for someone, then disappeared. When he returned to the house where he was staying, he told his host what he had seen, and then heard the tragic story of Charlotte Dymond for the first time. The stream he had crossed was where she had been murdered.

Devon: Chambercombe Manor: The Haunted Secret Room

It was in the year 1865 that the tenant farmer of the fine eleventh-century Chambercombe Manor, situated one mile south-east of the Devon town of Ilfracombe, between the sea and hills in the Chambercombe valley, discovered the secret room. For years the manor house had been haunted by mysterious cries and noises and the figure of a woman walking along the corridor, in and out of 'the Lady Jane Grey bedroom', through the Victorian bedroom, along the passage to the chapel, through the Great Hall and out into the cobbled courtyard, where it disappeared. The sinister and gruesome story of this ghost has been a mystery for countless years and remains unsolved even to this day.

The very earliest record of Chambercombe Manor was in the time of Edward the Confessor, and in the twelfth century it was owned by the Champernownes, then passing through distinguished families, including the Bonvilles, Greys, Sydneys and Gorges. Its most distinguished guest was the ill-fated Lady Jane Grey, whose father, Henry, Duke of Suffolk, had owned a considerable part of the manor lands, and came as a friend of Sir Henry Champernowne. She was executed by beheading in 1554 after reigning in 1553 for only nine days. A bedroom above the Great Hall, next to the secret room, is named after her. It contains a splendid Tudor four-poster bed and her coat of arms.

Towards the end of the sixteenth century the Gorges family were in possession and gave the title deeds to the vicar of Ilfracombe, vested in trustees. They sold the lands, known as 'Ropers', in several parcels to various farmers; thus they passed from their previous high estate. It remained a farmhouse until 1976 and is now open to the public.

The manor house at Gaulden, near Taunton in Somerset, seen from one of the beautiful small gardens created by the owners

Brockley Court with its adjacent church, home of the Smyth-Pigott family who were forced to abandon it because of the terrifying visitations

The now deserted and abandoned Woodchester Park mansion near Stroud in Gloucestershire, isolated in its valley of many ghosts

The beautiful old manor house of the Baring-Gould family at Lew Trenchard in Devon, constantly visited by 'Old Madam'

New College chapel, Oxford, showing an entrance doorway to the chapel where Dr Lumsden saw a ghostly figure

The monks' refectory at Hurley Priory, the haunted portion on the right, where a spectre has lately been seen

The entrance gate to Bodmin gaol where the Lightfoot brothers were hanged for murdering Neville Norway, the last public hanging in the town

The legendary bloody footstep in Smithills Hall, Bolton, of George Marsh, who was burnt at the stake as a Protestant martyr in 1555

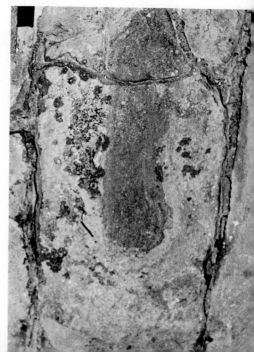

The eccentric Squire Butler of the Abbey House, Barnwell in
Cambridgeshire, whose spirit was dreaded by local children

Chetwynd Hall in Shropshire where the apparition of Madam
Pigott haunts the Hall and the surrounding countryside

Bouley Bay in Jersey where legend says the cries of the
Tombelenes can still be heard

The old manor house at Ville au Roi in Guernsey, once occupied
by the evil bailiff Gaultier de la Salle

Lady Anne's Tower at St Donat's Castle, Llantwit Major in Wales, haunted by the ghost of Lady Stradling

The farmer who first discovered the secret room had been for some time pestered by his wife to do something about the leaking roof. One summer day, when his wife had gone off early to market in Ilfracombe, he took a ladder and began climbing towards the chimney-stack, when he discovered, to his astonishment, what looked like the outline of a window which obviously belonged to a room he had never seen, though he had lived at the manor farm for some years.

He at once began to make further investigations, beginning on the brickwork surrounding the window, until he had made a hole large enough to look through, only to see a dark interior of what might have been a storehouse, though he had never been aware of the existence of such a room. He then came down from the ladder and went carefully over the inside of the whole house. He noticed unusual markings on the wall between Lady Jane Grey's room and the next room, so faint that neither he nor his wife had ever seen them. He at once fetched a pickaxe, and his work soon revealed what seemed to be a wall which was solid but which yielded to the heavy blows he gave it; continuing, with mounting excitement, thinking there might be buried treasure, he made a hole large enough to look through. At that moment his wife came back from market and, her curiosity overcoming her anger at the dust and fallen brickwork all over the floor, she watched him continue until he had made an aperture large enough to insert his head, then his shoulders, and finally big enough for his body to be able to enter. He told his wife to fetch candles, for the room was pitch dark, oppressive and smelling of damp and must. At last, holding their candles, the two wormed their way in, stunned at what they saw.

The light from the flickering candles revealed a long, narrow, low-ceilinged room. The tattered shreds of what must once have been magnificent tapestry hung from the walls. There were a wardrobe, table and chairs, all rotting away with damp and age, while the whole centre of the room was occupied by a magnificent black oak four-poster bed. The once splendid hangings were shrouded with dense cobwebs that also covered almost the whole room, which reeked of damp and rot. Thick dust covered the floor, so that the two made no sound as they moved apprehensively towards the bed, fearful of disturbing the hangings. A very thin light filtered through the pane of the enclosed window frame the farmer had first discovered. Finally, urged on by his wife, who did not dare move, the farmer slowly drew back the heavy bed curtains.

A most hideous shriek came from his wife. There on a pillow, yellow with age, lay a grinning skull. On the crimson coverlet lay a bony arm, and skeleton fingers clutched at the linen sheet, the rest of the skeleton body hidden under the linen. The tension was broken by the heavy fall of the farmer's wife as she fainted from the shock of what she had seen. The farmer revived her as best he could, and both of them scrambled out of the room and into the courtyard, where he at once summoned the farmhands to help him fill up the great aperture he had made in the wall, so that it could never be opened again. What he and his wife had witnessed was unforgettable, but, if he felt that by sealing up the wall again, this was the end of the matter, it was only because he could never have realized that what they had seen was to become one of the outstanding legends and mysteries of the folklore of Devonshire.

That same night the farmer was awakened by his wife, who, not surprisingly, told him that she felt ill. He at once got up and went over to the window to open it. He saw with wonder that the whole countryside was flooded by brilliant moonlight, outlining every single detail of the house and courtyard. Suddenly he became transfixed by what he saw below him, for there were figures of men rushing up and down, gesticulating and pointing out to sea and back again to the farmhouse. Two of them bent over what looked like a heavy barrel they pushed forward, whilst others were waving their arms and moving their mouths as if shouting orders. The farmer was so terrified that he slammed the window shut, rushed back to bed and lay beside his wife, trembling all over, pulling the coverlet over both of them. It was only then that he realized that what he had seen were not real figures but ghosts, for they were all noiseless; there had been no sounds of a barrel being bumped and rocked over the cobbled courtyard. He was convinced that this was a punishment he had brought on himself by discovering and opening the secret room with its appalling sight. The two decided to leave the farm and never come back. They leased it to a neighbouring farmer as soon as possible and, without giving any reason for going, left Chambercombe, never to return.

The explanation of the ghosts was that at some time during the early part of the nineteenth century a secret passage had been discovered leading from the manor house to Hele beach, about half a mile away, constantly used by smugglers and wreckers for depositing their loot and plunder, chiefly brandy for the owners and tenants. This must have been known to the farmer who discovered the secret room.

The legend of the skeleton on the bed in the secret room is probably the most controversial in the folklore of Devonshire. It is generally agreed, however, that it was that of Kate Oatway, daughter of William and Ellen Oatway. William was the son of Alexander Oatway, a renowned smuggler and wrecker, who had bought Chambercombe Farm when the Gorges' land was sold in parcels. One story suggests that it was Alexander Oatway who lured a ship onto the rocks by false lanterns, found one of the survivors, who was thought to be a titled and wealthy Spanish lady, and brought her up the secret passage to the farm, where he robbed her and, to avoid any suspicion, walled her up in the secret room and left her to starve to death.

Another legend says that it was not he but his son William who carried out this inhuman killing. He once followed his father, against strict orders, to see what he did at night, discovering it was smuggling and, worse still, wrecking. His furiously angry father sent him, his wife and his daughter Kate first to Tavistock, then to Lundy Island. After his father's death William took over Chambercombe Farm and was not himself averse to wrecking, so prevalent in those days along the whole coast.

One night there was a terrible wreck of a ship lured onto the dangerous rocks near Hele beach which William, like so many others, had watched with equally divided anxiety and hope for plunder. He noticed that one survivor had been thrown out of the ship onto the rocks. Going forward to investigate, his lantern revealed the body of a woman, her face and head almost mutilated beyond identification. She was sodden, but rich clothes and the jewels on her fingers flashed brilliantly. He gave her some brandy but she was only half conscious. He was a strong man and was easily able to carry her through the secret passage leading to the farm. His wife, Ellen, came at once to meet him and burst into tears as he laid the body down on a couch. Even through her tears, however, she saw the jewels. Then, lifting her up again, William carried her upstairs to a small room between the Lady Jane Grey bedroom and what is now the Victorian Room. It must at one time have been a dressing-room, for it was richly furnished. There he laid her on the bed and asked his wife to undress her while he fetched some things and changed his clothes.

When he came back, his wife had put the woman to bed and had laid all the jewellery out for him to see. There were diamond rings, a case of jewels in a handkerchief she had tied round her waist, a gold watch and chain and a gold necklace, all of which she had evidently gathered together when the ship was inevitably going to be wrecked in the heavy seas. The face of the woman was almost obliterated, yet even so Ellen told her husband that she seemed in some extraordinary way to resemble their daughter Kate; William did not agree and even became angry when Ellen showed him a piece of the jewellery stamped with the letter W – Kate had married a rich Irishman when quite young, years earlier, and had become Kate Wallis.

Early the next morning a villager named Roley, who had watched the wreck with Oatway, called to ask if he was all right, as he had not been seen the night before except by a seaman, who thought he had seen him carrying something heavy which might have been a survivor. He was assured that that was not true and went away again, though not absolutely convinced. A few days later another and totally unexpected visitor arrived at the farm. He was the skipper of the wrecked ship, to say that one of his seamen had been saved, as well as his first mate, and had been cared for at the local inn; the skipper had been told that someone had seen Mr Oatway carrying a heavy burden which might have been yet another survivor, and he had come to make sure. He had had quite an important lady passenger under his charge.

'Who was she?' asked Oatway.

'A lady from the north of Ireland, sir, going with us to Bristol. She knew all the coast off by heart as we came along, and we would have landed her, but the sea was so high. Were you expecting a visitor, sir?'

'You knew her name, of course?'

'A name familiar to you, sir, I've reason to believe.'

'Wallis?'

'Yes, sir.'

It must have been then that, with such suspicion in the village, though no actual proof, the farmer and his wife were forced to seal up the room in the way it was found some 150 years later and may be seen today through a small glass pane. As additional evidence, Oatway was said to have had a number of local debts which the valuable jewellery would have helped to pay off. It has also been reported that they sold up the farm, that Ellen died of grief shortly afterwards, that William lived until he was seventy and left a full confession before his death. This was discovered behind a fireplace in a cottage whose owners were doing repairs.

Standing in the outer courtyard, one can see the exact spot where the secret room was revealed. If anyone can still feel the horror of Kate Oatway's death, it is diminished by the very attractive gardens, most especially the rose garden, the herb garden and the very beautiful water gardens, set amidst four acres of Devon countryside.

Devon: Lew Trenchard: The Extraordinary Ghost

One of the most remarkable phantoms in the history of ghosts is surely that of Margaret Gould, known to all when alive and dead as 'Old Madam'. Who else but this formidable woman, who died in the family home at Lew Trenchard in Devon, could appear, as she did, half an hour after her death, thereafter continually haunting the house, the estates and surrounding countryside?

It is entirely due to her descendant Sabine Baring-Gould that Old Madam's story came to be widely known when he wrote his *Early Reminiscences*. He was no less remarkable a character, multi-lingual at the age of fifteen, assistant housemaster at Hurstpierpoint College in Sussex, inexhaustible traveller, author of over 150 books, rector of Lew Trenchard and an avaricious researcher and collector of folklore, dying at the family home at Lew Trenchard in 1924.

When Margaret's husband, William Drake Gould, died in 1766, the estates passed to their son Edward, who was a rake and lost a good deal of the property; he would eventually have lost it all if his mother had not taken out a lease to prevent him. When their daughter Margaret was married to Charles Baring, 'Old Madam' went to stay with them at their home near Exmouth. One Sunday they took her to a Quaker meeting instead of church, as she expected, and she was so indignant that she cut them out of her Will in favour of their son William, grandfather of Sabine Baring-Gould.

When the rents had been collected from the estate farmers, 'Old Madam' would put all the guineas into saddle-bags, mount her horse and, escorted by a manservant on another horse, set out on a long ride for the bank in Exeter. When asked one day if she were not afraid of highwaymen, she replied that highwaymen were more likely to fear her, and exhibited the pistol which she always carried. Amongst her many eccentricities were her methods for preventing burglars coming down the chimneys by inserting heavy iron bars with the spikes upwards in order to impale the burglars.

On 10 April 1795 she died in her favourite high-backed chair, refusing to take to her bed. A groom was sent to inform her daughter, who returned sitting pillion on the horse, holding tight to the strap round the groom's waist to prevent being unhorsed. Margaret's husband refused to attend the funeral since he had been cut out of Old Madam's Will.

When she died, the shutters of the window slammed open as if they had been struck by a high wind, making such a crash that the cook came rushing in, frightened that there were burglars in the house. Half an hour later, one of the servants saw her standing under a walnut tree in the garden and was terrified. It was her first appearance as a ghost.

Murray, in his *Handbook of Devon*, states that her ghost was always in white, with long hair, '...sparkling as if covered with water drops. A true White Lady.' She began almost at once to haunt the avenue of her old house, but most frequently the beautiful Long Gallery, where at night more than one person heard the clicking of her high-heeled shoes as she proceeded with her customary measured tread. She was seen walking along a corridor and opening a door as if to admit someone, then closing it after he or she had entered, before vanishing, though the door was locked. One summer night Baring-Gould's sister, hearing her steps, decided to follow her and saw her pass through two doors before disappearing. One daughter said that when she was a child she had seen a lady in blue who came into the nursery, bent over her, looked at her and even sat beside her bed, though never frightening her. Another daughter, when ill as a child, was being looked after by a trained nurse who had dozed off. There came a knock at the door and a voice saying, 'It is time for her medicine', but no one was there at the door.

When little Beatrice Baring-Gould was ill, cutting teeth

and with whooping-cough, the nurse was not very alert, and the child's mother decided to sleep in the bedroom. In the middle of the night the mother rushed to Sabine Baring-Gould in the room where Old Madam died, declaring she could not sleep because of people tramping up and down the stairs carrying something. He tried to soothe his wife. Next day, not realizing that the child was so ill, they made a call, and on returning the mother fetched the child, who was already dressed, and took her into the library. Hearing a sudden call, Baring-Gould ran to the library to find that the child had died on her mother's knees. Her coffin had to be carried down the staircase from which the noises had come on the previous night.

Old Madam's ghost was often seen by Lew and Bratton people standing by a stream on very dark nights, dressed in white and 'shimmering', either bending to cup her hands with water, which trickled through her fingers, or combing her long hair with a silver comb. One man who saw her when he was returning from market was so scared that he took to his heels, afraid the ghost would follow him home.

One of her most astounding appearances was when she was seen by a man who had just returned from America. He had left Lew during Old Madam's lifetime many years before and was then living at Holdstrong. He had hired a horse at Tavistock to ride to Galford, and it was bright moonlight when he rode through the Lew valley, on the left of which he noticed a ploughed field where a plough was standing, on which, to his astonishment, he saw a lady in white satin with long hair floating over her shoulders. Her face was uplifted and her eyes were staring directly upwards at the moon. So clear was her face that at once he recognized Old Madam even after the long years and called out to her, 'A very good night to you, Madam.' She bowed her head and waved her hand in recognition, he noticing the sparkle and glitter of the diamond rings she wore on her fingers, and he thought how well she looked after the long years. When he arrived at Galford, he told his relatives what he had seen. 'What do you think? I have seen that strange Madam Gould sitting on a plough, this time of night, looking at the moon.' His relatives stared at him in a stunned silence until one said: 'Madam was buried seven days ago in Lew church.'

Not long after this, Old Madam made another visitation, this time to one of her former orchards. An old woman who related the event to Baring-Gould told him that, when she was young, the trees in the orchard being covered with ripe apples, she had shaken a tree and begun to gather up the tumbled apples, filling her pockets with as many as she could. Suddenly she looked up to see Old Madam standing before her and pointing an accusing finger at her and the apple she was holding. Terrified, the woman dropped it and ran as fast as she could to a gap in the hedge where a slate slab served as a bridge. Once again she was confronted by Old Madam, who had moved faster than she and was now looking at her very sternly, pointing at her pockets bulging with stolen apples. Not until she had emptied her pockets did Old Madam vanish.

Old Madam's ghost was often seen by various people in different parts of her former estates, walking over Galford Down or by the path to the old church and the Dew Pond, pausing there for a moment before passing on. A coming-out ball was once given in the Long Gallery for a Baring-Gould daughter, after which several of the guests were curious to know who the dark lady was in a lace dress and with grey hair, moving in and out of the dancers without a word to anyone. One gentleman said he had seen her standing under a portrait of Margaret Ballard (Old Madam's maiden name) and had noticed how alike they were; though the lady was much older, the resemblance was very close. There was no old lady at that ball; all the guests were young people.

When the rector of Bratton invited the Baring-Goulds to high tea, the cook, on hearing who were his guests, refused to cook for them, as she said Old Madam had been the cause of her brother's breaking his leg when he was returning from Tavistock one night. He had seen her, all in white, near the mine-shaft and was so alarmed that he scrambled over the hedge and fell!

Baring-Gould also tells of a certain Mr Twiggs who, staying as a guest in his house, came down dressed for dinner and, since he was the only guest, was astonished to see two figures in the drawing-room. One was sitting in an armchair with its back towards him, so that he could only see a gentleman with either a wig or powdered hair. Opposite him sat an elderly lady in a satin dress. Not wishing to disturb them, he went back through the dining-room, where his host was, and asked him who were the other two guests. Baring-Gould went at once to the drawing-room, but it was empty. He then remembered that he had been told long before that it was the custom on Saturday and Sunday evenings for Old Madam to invite Parson Elford of Lew church to visit her for a chat. In church, Old Madam and the clerk had been the only two of the congregation who could read, so when a psalm was given out, the clerk would say: 'Let Madam and I sing to the praise and glory of God.'

Baring-Gould's theory on Old Madam was that a spectral transference had been made from Susanna Gould, an ancestor, who had married rather against her father's wishes and, reaching the house from the church after the wedding, had dropped dead in her white bridal gown. There was no reason at all for Old Madam to be all in white.

Her last appearance was the most terrifying of all. It happened in 1832, thirty-seven years after her death, when a carpenter who was employed in the repair of Lew Trenchard church was curious enough to examine the vault containing the coffins of Old Madam and her husband and noticed that her coffin lid was slightly displaced. As he moved forward to adjust it, she sat up, opened her eyes and rose to her feet. The church was filled with light from her figure. In terror he fled but was even more scared when she followed him out of the church, down the path and into the avenue. So luminous was her spectral figure that he could see his shadow before him as he ran. He reached his home, opened the door and rushed up to the bedroom where his infirm wife was asleep and jumped in beside her. She also saw the blinding light surrounding the figure, 'so bright she could have seen a pin lying on the floor'.

What is so extraordinary about Old Madam's daylight

and night visitations is the intensity of her appearances at the home, farms and lands she had fought so hard to win back from near-bankruptcy, with a strength of purpose and determination rarely seen in the village. She was never cruel, never unkind, never did anyone any harm. She was a very remarkable ghost indeed and might well turn up again in Lew Trenchard.

Somerset: Brockley, near Bristol: The Dangerous Ghost of Brockley Court

There can be no doubt whatsoever that the ghost haunting Brockley Court was a dangerous one, and its authenticity has been documented in the archives of the Society for Psychical Research, who have generously allowed me to see their record. The whole series of events was witnessed and recorded by members of the family owners and their guests.

Brockley Court is a splendid old manor house standing within spacious grounds in the village of Brockley, between Bristol airport and Clevedon. It was in the possession of the distinguished Smyth-Pigott family for three centuries, first purchased in 1661 by the Rt.Hon. Thomas Pigott, and was held until the early twentieth century, when they were driven out by the ghost.

The house had always had a reputation for its haunting: no local person would ever work there, nor go near it at night, and the family always had to bring their own staff of servants. For more than sixty years reports and rumours circulated about its ghost, and at one time it was empty for eighteen years. In addition to the Court's problems, the adjacent Brockley Combe had its own ghosts to deal with.

The first meticulously detailed account of the appearance of the ghost was given in an interview with John Smyth-Pigott, who related his personal experience on 22 or 23 August 1900. He was reading in bed before sleeping, when something made him look up to see in astonishment a figure standing by the door leading into the Arch Room. A counterpane thrown over the rail at the foot of the bed prevented him from seeing the whole figure, only the upper part. Its hands were stretched out before it, with the palms downwards in an imploring, preventive gesture, but it did not move. Then, advancing around and passing the bed, it disappeared through the door leading into the passage. It was so near to him that he could see the whole figure, dressed in a dark material with a white choker or lace at the neck and what looked like a small rapier at its left side. It was only a little later that he realized that it resembled the figure of his great-great-great-uncle John Pigott, whose portrait was in the house. He felt convinced of this by the white choker and the hair brushed back over a high forehead. The face of the figure, however, was vacant and expressionless. More astonished than alarmed, he kept the candles burning but passed a sleepless night.

He told his uncle the next morning of the apparition, but he ridiculed the story until his nephew mentioned the resemblance to the portrait.

That night John slept in the Green Room once more; he was uneasy but not nervous, not expecting the figure to appear again. It was about eleven o'clock when he began to undress, and just at the moment he was taking off his tie, he felt there was something behind him. Turning suddenly, he saw the figure again, this time moving towards the door leading to the passage, where it vanished, though the door was not open. It all happened so swiftly that he had no time to notice details of the figure as before. He rushed at once towards his uncle's room, meeting him at the end of the passage. He told his uncle he had just seen the ghost, and his uncle said he had also seen it.

From that time he slept in his uncle's room, keeping it secret from both his family and the servants, although his brother Bernard experienced a visitation – which will be related later. About a fortnight later Jack (as he was known in the family) was lying in bed (a sofa at the foot of his uncle's bed) when he felt himself being lifted from a sleeping position to a rising, upright one by what must have been a very strong man, who seemed to be grasping at the lappets of his nightdress. After a few seconds he was released from its hold, and his body fell back onto his pillow. Now fully awake, he immediately saw the figure. In the darkness of the room he first became conscious of dark eyes looking at him and realized that the figure was luminous, white, not blue, and was either kneeling or sitting by his bed. It was again only half the figure that he saw, and it remained for almost a minute staring at him. What he did notice was the mouth: it was ugly; the corners drooped. Then the figure seemed to melt away rather than move suddenly.

Yet another visitation has been graphically described by Mr Smyth-Pigott:

I was in the Arch Room in bed reading, as was also my uncle. My bed, a small one, stood at the foot of my uncle's large bed. There were at least 2 candles burning and probably three. We were both wide awake, only having been in bed some 5 minutes. I suddenly heard my uncle's book close with a bang. I sat up to look over on to his bed, and saw his arms stretched out in front of him with the hands clenched. He was struggling and trying to draw himself back. Quite suddenly he fell out of bed head foremost on to the floor, with his legs up in the air quite close to my bed. I then saw him being dragged along the floor round the projecting closet towards the door leading into the passage. He was being pulled on his stomach along the floor by the wrists – or apparently by the wrists, as his arms were in the air above his head.

Hardly knowing what I was doing I rushed out of the door that leads through the powder closet and green room into the passage. Arrived in the passage I saw that the other door, towards which my uncle had been dragged was shut so I ran back into the Arch Room, where I found my uncle lying on the floor by the door in an exhausted condition. I raised him up and got him back to bed. He then and there said that he had seen the figure standing by one of the pillars, which is close to the head of my bed; that after standing there a few moments, it came forward, seized him by the wrists, and then dragged him in the manner described. He saw the figure the whole time, and it kept its eyes fixed on him. After a few minutes we both went downstairs to fetch a priest, Father Troake, who was staying in the house. He came up and blessed the room – after which we went to bed again, leaving our candles burning. About an hour later, neither of us having slept, the figure suddenly appeared at the foot of my bed by another pillar. When my uncle was dragged out of my bed, I saw no figure – but we both saw it now at the same time and in the same place. My uncle came down to the end of his bed and we caught hold of each other's hand and began to talk to the ghost. We asked it several questions. I asked it why it came several times. But the ghost did not reply to any question, except when I asked 'Why are you here?' It replied: 'This is my home'. My uncle heard nothing, but I heard the words spoken clearly in a deep and expressionless voice. A second or two after speaking, it disappeared.

Mr Smyth-Pigott, in an earlier part of the interview he gave, had stated that the appearances of the ghost were so frequent that he could not detach them one from another with sufficient accuracy. He said:

I used to wake up and find the face only within sometimes a yard or less of my own face – sometimes the full figure by my bedside. Sometimes while I was watching the face, it would recede and then disappear. No sound ever accompanied the appearances. The features appeared the same on all occasions. It was a malicious, horrible face. The last occasion on which I saw the figure during my summer stay at Brockley Court was 3 or 4 days before we left, which we did on [?] Sept.23.

Mr Bernard Smyth-Pigott was also consulted about his experiences, and they too were extremely frightening. He had been told about the ghost by his brother; two days later he was sleeping in the schoolroom with his younger brother, Rushcombe. He awoke about 1.30 feeling ill; getting up and turning into the passage, he saw 'John' standing by the Green Room door, dressed as in the family portrait, with a rapier, although there was no rapier in the portrait. His description of the ghost was the same as his brother Jack's had been, but this time the spectre seemed to be talking, though no sounds came. Bernard was petrified. The candle fell out of the candlestick he held in his hand, and he bolted back to his bedroom. Next morning he went away to make a visit to some friends.

Some six or seven days later Bernard returned, sleeping in the same bedroom as before, this time with his uncle for companion. Being nervous, he kept awaking, there being a little light in the room from bright moonlight through the shutters. About a minute before he saw the ghost, he found himself bathed in perspiration, with extreme body-tingling. It came *through* a cupboard and to the foot of his uncle's bed, then disappeared *through* the door. He woke his uncle and they opened the door, but nothing was there.

He saw nothing further for a week and then experienced the same sensations before seeing the white figure. This time, in full moonlight, he was able to see the piercing bright eyes, though not the lower part of the face.

The family were once again at Brockley Court in December, presumably for Christmas celebrations. This time Mr John Smyth-Pigott had brought with him Mr Marius Bode, of Keble College, Oxford, who was extremely anxious to see the ghost. They were sleeping in the Arch Room, his friend in the larger bed, he in the smaller. He was awakened by being raised in bed and found the ghost behind the head of his bed. It moved round to Bode's bed and disappeared into the wall. Bode was still sleeping and seems to have missed what he came to see!

Brockley Court is now a residential home for the elderly but, in spite of obvious alterations, the author and his wife were courteously conducted by Mr Groves to see the Arch Room, which is still intact. Perhaps the most interesting part of the visit was to go into the lovely little church, only a few yards away from the mansion (where the key is kept). It has a splendid Norman door, thirteenth-century stained glass windows, box pews and a remarkable large room for the Pigotts right opposite the pulpit, containing period chairs, a huge armchair and a wide-open fireplace, all ensuring peace and slumbers for the customary three-hour sermon of those times. There are three hatchments of the family, the finest to Colonel John Pigott, who died 1727.

Somerset: *Tolland, near Taunton:*
The Ghosts of Gaulden Manor

From the moment of arrival and entry into Gaulden
Manor, it is almost impossible to believe in ghosts, such is
the peace and quiet of this charming house, open to the
public at certain times of the year, though privately owned
by Mr and Mrs James Le Gendre Starkie. They welcome
guests and personally act as guides around the house and
its very beautiful gardens. Yet legend and folklore are
strong, and ghosts there are in plenty.

Almost 800 years have passed since King John gave
Gaulden-in-Tolland to Taunton Priory with all its lands,
rents and privileges. Its most famous occupant after the
Dissolution of the Monasteries by Henry VIII was James
Turberville of Bere Regis in Dorset, appointed Bishop of
Exeter by 'Bloody' Mary. (The family has been immortalized by Thomas Hardy in his famous novel *Tess of the
d'Urbervilles*.) James Turberville was one of the six
courageous bishops who refused to take the Oath of
Supremacy imposed upon them by Queen Elizabeth in
1559, for which he was imprisoned in the dreaded Tower
of London. There he remained for four years and was only
then released upon condition that he remain under the
care and watchful eyes of the Bishop of London.

'This Bishop Turberville,' wrote Fuller in his *Worthies of
England*, 'carries something of trouble in his name though
nothing but mildness and meekness in his nature, the
privacy of whose life caused the obscurity of his death.' It
is believed the bishop came to Gaulden for peace and
tranquillity, probably leasing the house. As Fuller wrote,
he died in obscurity, his place of burial unknown, but it is
more than likely he was buried in the family vault at Bere
Regis. His memory is immortalized in the superb plaster
frieze in the Great Hall at Gaulden, which has been dated

c.1570, but it is also thought that it may have been done in memory of his great-uncle by John Turberville, who bought the house in 1639. The frieze depicts religious scenes, symbols and events in the life of the bishop, such as the Scales of Justice and the Tower, followed by the Virgin and Child triumphant. The family arms are above the fireplace, with the arms of Sir Robert Turberville and Sir Richard Turberville on each side. There is also a handsome Turberville bedroom and a private chapel.

The most authentic of the many ghost stories of Gaulden Manor is that of the spectral Turberville Coach. This was a large and lumbering seventeenth-century family coach, which is stated to have started from Wool-bridge manor house (now an hotel) in Wool, Dorset, formerly the Turberville home. It would set out, drawn by four horses, at sunset and travel fast to Bere Regis, another family house, then on to Melcombe Bingham, into whose owner's family they had married and which had a beautiful garden. (Queen Elizabeth I is said to have planted the yew hedge, now considered the finest in England, twenty feet high and twenty feet wide.) On Midsummer Eve the coach would set out for Gaulden Manor, probably via Sherborne and somewhere near Taunton. There it could be heard driving up to the front door. The phantom coach could only be seen by anyone with Turberville blood and came as a warning of death.

Ghostly footsteps have been heard by Mr and Mrs Starkie on the main staircase and in the passage many times, but they have never known the cause or seen anyone. Nor have they been able to solve the problem of the loud and distinct knock on the bedroom door. The knocks occurred late at night or very early in the morning. Whatever the cause, the ghosts are treated as friendly and are accepted as such.

Most of the ghost information has come to the owners from visitors to the manor or from hearsay or legends passed down through generations by word of mouth, as all too many unauthenticated stories have always been. A grey lady has often been seen sitting by the fireplace, and another woman, a small one, haunts the front stairs. A previous owner of Gaulden always kept a small room empty and locked because it was haunted by a ghostly lady. In order to avoid constant questioning, he kept it so, but gave no further information as to what he had seen.

My own very slight disturbance came when entering what was once the Chapel, but it was in no way unfriendly, rather the reverse. This is now a small room with a Tudor fireplace and a plaster frieze similar to the one in the Great Hall, with angels and cherubs. The entrance to the room is on the right-hand side of the fireplace in the Great Hall. One visitor told the owners that she had felt something very unpleasant in the Great Hall but could give no explanation for her feelings. The owners then recalled that a visitor had once told them that as he entered the room he saw three Cavaliers standing in front of the carved panels dividing the Great Hall and the Chapel. They were covered in blood, and he categorically refused to enter the Chapel.

Some confirmation of this story came from another visitor, a schoolteacher, who said that in fact a great battle had taken place nearby during the Civil Wars; he thought it probable that the Cavaliers either were billeted at Gaulden or had taken refuge there for safety, wounded or actually dying, and that, even though 300 years had passed, their ghosts still haunted the Great Hall. Cromwell's men were at Gaulden Manor for over a week on one occasion.

Further confirmation came from a visitor in 1983 who suddenly halted, saying that the hair at the back of his head pricked and he was sure something had happened there. A former housekeeper told the present owners that she had once seen a monk in the Turberville bedroom, but did not seem to have been frightened.

The very beautiful gardens do not appear to be disturbed by any ghost monks, if there are any, as has been reported. The prior of Taunton came here to collect the rents, and many monks are supposed to be buried in the garden, possibly that named 'the Monk's Garden'. There are, in addition, 'the Secret Garden', 'the Bog Garden', 'the Elizabethan Herb Garden', 'the Bishop's Garden' and one or two more already created or being created by Mrs Starkie. A large, beautiful pond, clearly viewed from the Secret Garden, would have held all the fish a monastery would have required. There have also been reports of two secret passages. One leads from Gaulden towards Wiveliscombe, another to Grove farm, which was formerly a nunnery.

One comes away from Gaulden accepting all the ghosts because they are friendly ones, except the three Cavaliers, and if there are monks in the gardens, they could add even more to their peace and serenity, for that is the memory one has of this house, set in some of the loveliest countryside in England. One does not have to believe in the supernatural at all to enjoy such moments of peace and quiet in either the house or its gardens. One only wants to return there and enjoy it once again.

Somerset: Watchet: The Phantom Train

Ghost trains are rarer than any other type of manifest-ations; in fact, one would have difficulty in finding phantom trains in the many ghost stories published. Yet not one but many local people have seen the West Somerset Mineral Railway ghost train at Kentsford, between Washford and Watchet. Not only do they claim to have seen the train but they have also heard the voices of Edwardian children returning from their holidays at Minehead. They were first heard laughing happily between 1901 and 1910, and even during World War I. It was only after 1917, when the line was closed and the rails all ripped up to be sent to munitions factories, that the first of a continuous number of sightings of the phantom train was rumoured during World War II, and disbelieved.

The first accurate and revealing identity of the type of train was recorded by a local historian, who, by his own researches and careful checking, had discovered that the phantom train could have only been the tank engine and wagons involved in a bad accident almost a century before.

His search through railway records revealed that an accident had taken place at Kentsford, near Watchet, on 22 August 1857, when an engine left Roadwater with a truck carrying about thirty labourers returning to Watchet for their pay. On reaching Washford, Henry Giles, the crossing-keeper, held up his flag and stopped the train, warning the driver not to proceed, as a coal train was expected shortly from Watchet.

John James, the assistant engineer, was riding on the engine. After close-questioning the crossing-keeper and because he had urgent letters to post, he decided they should go on. Giles climbed onto the buffer beam, and the train proceeded at 20 mph, whistling loudly as a warning of its approach. On rounding a curve at Kentsford, they suddenly saw the coal train about 200 yards away but were unable to avoid a head-on collision. Both engines were damaged, one off the line, the other left derelict. A month passed before another engine could replace them. Giles was killed instantly, James and another dying of their wounds later; several others were severely injured and badly scalded by escaping steam. The coroner, after a hearing lasting three days, brought in a verdict of manslaughter against James. The accident and inquest were fully reported in the *Taunton Chronicle* of 26 August and 2 September 1857.

The most extraordinary part of this story is that nearly a hundred years passed before the ghost train came to be talked about more and more. Many local people, encouraged by what they heard from others, readily divulged their own experiences. Often at night the sound of a passing train, its whistle blowing all the time, was heard. Others had heard the cries of wounded people who were passengers on the train. Some had seen the lighted engine cab from the fire burning brightly as the stoker shovelled the coal in to keep the speed of 20 mph maintained. It all seems improbable when one considers that some thirty years had gone by since the rails were ripped up.

Nevertheless, a few years after the war a postman and his friend, who were both in the local brass band and had obviously heard about the phantom train, decided to have a look for themselves. One night after they had finished band practice they were just about to cross over the bridge towards some abandoned brickworks when they both saw a tank engine drawing trucks soundlessly reaching the bridge and vanishing. Such was their astonishment and fright that they decided to tell no one what they had seen, for fear of being jeered at. After a while, however, they were so convinced of what they had seen that they told a reporter on the local paper, and the story was headlined. It was only then that several other people confirmed that they, too, had seen the train but were also reluctant to tell anyone because of being laughed at.

Shortly after the article appeared, a man who was deeply interested in the occult came to see the two men, was convinced of their sincerity and truth and arranged that they should all three make vigils at night, to see if the ghost train would appear. The first two nights nothing was seen and the investigator, as he considered himself to be, wanted to give up, but he was persuaded to give it another chance, and all three set out for the third night.

It was a bitterly cold February night, and between two and three o'clock in the morning, their bodies frozen, their patience running out, one of them suddenly gave a cry as he saw a lighted engine cab ahead of them and the clear shape of an approaching train travelling at an estimated 20 mph. As it approached the bridge, the investigator craned forward: the train passed below the bridge and vanished. In his excitement he had closed his eyes and could not believe what he had seen, but the others both said they had seen it. There was no longer any doubt that there was a phantom train, but the astonishing thing was that none of them had heard a sound. So certain were they all that they had seen the train that they swore an affidavit with the local solicitor, and the facts became front-page news in all the papers. Then all was silent. In spite of countless further vigils, even by press reporters, the ghost train was never seen again.

7 Northern Ireland

Curraghmore: The Warning and Prophetic Ghost

It is almost 300 years since the ghost of the Second Earl of Tyrone appeared to his childhood friend Lady Beresford, in October 1693, with a grim and prophetic warning that has made the story unique in the many considerable records of the supernatural. Its authenticity and documentation were first given by Lady Betty Cobbe in 1806, unfortunately since lost. The second version was in *Lord Halifax's Ghost Book*, 1827, the third account by the Reverend F. Lee in his *Glimpses in the Twilight*, 1884. Whilst all three accounts are reasonably similar, the dates differ greatly, with consequent confusion.

Lady Beresford was the wife of Sir Tristram Beresford. When she was a child, she and one John Power were constant companions and both convinced believers in Deism, the belief in a God without accepting revelation. When his father died in the Tower as a Jacobite prisoner, John became second Earl of Tyrone. The two devoted friends had made a mutual and solemn pact that whoever died first should appear to the other to declare what was the true religion. Until the time of his death three years later and after the marriage of Lady Beresford, the two had continued their visits to each other until the very last one when Lord Tyrone appeared to her on that October night, not as a living person but as a ghost, to fulfil his promise.

Lady Beresford was very startled to awake and find her dear friend sitting beside her bed. She was terrified when she heard him speak and declare that he had been permitted to appear and to assure her that revealed religion was the true and only religion by which he and she could be saved. He then told her she was 'in child with a son', who, it was decreed, was to marry his niece after Sir Tristram's death. He also told her that she would then marry a man who would make her life a misery, that in spite of his ill-treatment she would give him two daughters and a son and that she would die in her forty-seventh year.

She then interrupted him for the first time to ask if she could prevent this, to which he replied that, as she was a free agent, she could resist it by not being tempted to a second marriage but, as she well knew, her passions were strong and open to temptation. 'If, after this warning,' he said, 'you persist in infidelity, your lot in another world will be miserable indeed.' She then asked him if he was happy, to which he replied, 'Had it been otherwise I should not have been permitted to appear to you.'

Lady Beresford then demanded some evidence of his appearance, as she would not be able to prove it to others. One account says he offered to sign his name in her pocket-book, another says she declined his offer. He then waved his hands and, drawing aside the heavy crimson bed-hangings, thrust them through a large iron ring, something she herself was not strong enough to do. He then demanded that she hold out her hand and he would give her irrefutable proof that he had appeared that night. Lady Beresford's own words remain in all accounts: 'He touched my wrist with a hand as cold as marble and in a moment the sinews were shrunk up with every nerve with them. "Now," he abjured me, "let no mortal eye while you live behold that wrist. To see it would be sacrilege." He was silent and when I turned to him again he was gone. During the time I was conversing with him I was perfectly calm and collected but the moment he was gone I felt filled with horror.'

When she got up after a sleepless night, she first tried to release the bed-hangings but was physically unable to do so and left them for the servants to see. With extreme care and in great fear she bound her wrist with a black velvet bracelet and went down to breakfast. As she sat down, her husband noticed immediately her pale and distraught face, showing obvious signs of terror, and asked anxiously after her health. She replied that she felt perfectly well as usual. Then, seeing the black velvet bracelet, he asked if she had hurt her wrist. She replied: 'Nothing has happened, but had it, let me beg you, Sir Tristram, never to enquire the cause of my wearing this ribbon. You will never again see me without it. If it concerns you as a husband to know why I wear it I would tell you. I never in my life denied you a request but about this I must entreat you to forgive my silence and never urge me again on the subject.'

As if such a reply to his question were not enough, and as she still seemed nervous and anxious, she told him that there should be a letter announcing the death of Lord Tyrone and that she herself would be giving Sir Tristram a son. Twice she impatiently rang the bell to ask the servant if the postman had been, but he had not. Some time later he brought her a letter sealed with black wax. She handed it to her husband, who opened it. It was from Lord Tyrone's steward, announcing his master's death. Both her statements proved to be true, for nine months later she gave birth to a son. Seven years later Sir Tristram died.

In spite of Lord Tyrone's warning to her about a second marriage, Lady Beresford accepted a proposal made by Lieutenant-General Gorges, who made her life a misery from the start, just as she had been told. They parted for some time before he came back to give her two daughters and make her pregnant for the third time. According to Lady Cobbe's record, clear and detailed as it was, Lady Beresford gave birth to a son. One month later she invited her son and daughter by her first husband, Lady Cobbe herself and an old clergyman friend to come and celebrate her forty-eighth birthday, relieved as she was to have disproved the prophetic warning of Lord Tyrone that she would die in her forty-seventh year.

She had decided that at last she must inform those dearest to her of the whole series of warnings and prophecies the ghost of Lord Tyrone had made to her all those years previously, and in particular the reason she had for never removing the black ribbon from her wrist. She made them promise that after her death they must remove the ribbon from her wrist and see for themselves the positive truth of the mark the ghost had left and his threat of sacrilege if she removed it or told anyone the reason for wearing it.

It was only when she had finished this astonishing story that the clergyman reminded her that she was not, as she believed, forty-eight years old but in her forty-seventh year. He had christened her, he said, and had a record of the date of her birth. Lady Beresford paused for a long time, then asked them to leave so that she could compose herself after her ordeal of revealing a long-guarded secret. Some hour or two later her bedside bell rang violently, and when her family and friend rushed upstairs, they found her dead. When they obeyed her last request and unbound the black ribbon, they saw with their own eyes the withered nerves and sinews of the ghost hand of Lord Tyrone. His last prophecy had come true, for Lady Beresford had died in her forty-seventh year. Not long after her death her son, Marcus Beresford, married the niece of Lord Tyrone.

Thus every one of the ghost's warnings and prophecies had come to pass. In spite of much confusion of dates and facts from the three main authorities, this story is unique in the history of the supernatural and a real challenge to believers and disbelievers alike of such an apparition as the ghost of Lord Tyrone three centuries ago.

Londonderry: *The Radiant Boy*

According to Dr Korner, the German authority on spectral incidents, the apparition of a beautiful, naked, gentle boy with dazzling, gold-coloured hair enclosing his head like the halo of a saint, has been classified in ghost history as *The Radiant Boy*. Ancient Teutonic legends and folklore, deeply expressed as they are in a supernatural mysticism, regard this type of ghost – a luminous spirit – to be of ill omen because it is always connected with children murdered by their mother, who are supposed to appear every seven years in the place where they have first been seen, bringing their message of good and evil to the person they visit. Illogical as all this seems, it has passed into Scandinavian and Irish folklore and been accepted.

The first appearance of *The Radiant Boy* in Ireland was given in Cathleen Crowe's book *The night side of Nature*. The story was told to her by a member of the Marquis of Londonderry's family, whose authenticity she vouched for. The person visited by the ghost was Captain Robert Stewart, afterwards Viscount Castlereagh and later second Marquis of Londonderry. Towards the end of the eighteenth century, as a young man, he was quartered in Londonderry, when one day he decided to go shooting game. The morning started quite brightly, but as the afternoon came clouds began to gather, and by early evening heavy rain began to fall. By then the Captain had wandered quite a distance, and suddenly realized that he had lost his way in the thickly wooded countryside.

It was growing quite dark and the prospect of finding a path to lead him back grew dimmer and dimmer, when ahead of him at some distance he saw a lighted building and stumbled his way towards it, soaked to the skin, utterly demoralized and tired. He pulled on the heavy iron chain and heard the bell echoing in the house. He then heard footsteps and a butler opened the door, to whom the Captain handed his card and asked if he could see the master of the house. After some minutes two men came towards him, and the master, impressed by the Captain's rank, at once invited him in, telling the butler to find some dry clothes. He then apologized most profusely because his house was crammed with guests, some of them unknown to him, but lost and soaked as the Captain was, but assuring him that he would find somewhere for him to sleep that night. But first he must change, have a hot drink and something to eat, then mix with all the others until the gong sounded for dinner. He once again apologized that, as he was a widower, there was no lady to look after him. Turning to the butler who had come towards him, he told him to find a room somewhere in the house where the Captain could sleep.

The house was indeed crammed; the Captain soon found, after changing into dry clothes, that a very jolly party was in full swing, with whiskey seemingly flowing into glasses. Once again the master sought him out and after quite a long chat persuaded the Captain to stay on for another night or two, as many of the guests would be leaving in the morning. The Captain, only too pleased, promised him that he would. After dinner the party gradually went off to their rooms and the butler came to him to ask if he would like to follow him to the room in which he was to sleep. They wandered along dark passages and landings, up stairs and along other passages and landings, until they reached the room, where the butler bade him good night, hoping he would be able to sleep, regretting he could find no other room available, then left.

The room was completely devoid of any furniture. On the floor was a makeshift bed of sheets and blankets on a mattress. A candle burned on a stool but in the fireplace a blazing fire had been lighted, filling the room with warmth and light, a most welcome sight to the tired and exhausted Captain, who was in bed within minutes and fast asleep. How long he slept he never knew. He thought it might have been a couple of hours, but he awoke suddenly to see the whole room flooded with light. He sat up in bed rubbing his eyes, afraid that the room was on fire, instead of which he saw the grate was full of ashes from the fire that had died out. Then suddenly his body stiffened with fear.

Standing in the middle of the room he saw a vision of a young and most beautiful naked boy with hair like spun gold, his whole body surrounded by a dazzling radiance that filled the room with light. The luminous boy looked intensely at the Captain, before gliding slowly away towards the fireplace, where he vanished, leaving the now frightened Captain staring into the intense darkness, unable to move. In great discomfort, cold, irritable and finally angry, the Captain longed for the time when he could get up. He was convinced someone had played a rather unpleasant trick on him, a practical joke by another guest. Yet the vision of that beautiful boy standing in his aura of blinding light and his earnest, searching eyes as if he wanted to say something before he vanished, still haunted the Captain and greatly disturbed him.

When he finally got up and went down to breakfast only

his host and the butler were there. Both greeted him, but he made no answer, still angry and indignant at what he considered to have been a bad and distasteful joke for which he had been chosen to be the victim. It was only when his host asked him if he had slept well that he bluntly answered by saying he would be leaving after breakfast. There was a short silence before the host called the butler to the table.

'Hamilton,' he said, 'where did Captain Stewart sleep last night?'

'Well, sir,' the butler replied apologetically, 'you know the place was full. The gentlemen were even lying on the floor, three or four in a room, so I gave him the *Boy's Room*. But I made up a blazing fire for him and found a mattress and some blankets.'

'You were very wrong,' snapped the host. 'You know I have positively forbidden you to put anyone there and have ordered all the furniture to be removed from there to ensure it not being occupied.' Then, standing up, he invited the now astonished and puzzled Captain to come with him into the library. It was there that he disclosed the family secret of *The Radiant Boy*. Whomsoever saw him would rapidly rise to great fame and when he had reached the climax would die a violent death.

'I must tell you,' he concluded in an impressive voice, 'the record that has been kept of his appearances every seven years in that room have confirmed the truth of his silent warning and I am deeply concerned that the butler should have disobeyed my instructions.'

It was then the Captain's turn to apologize for his behaviour but he assured his host that his prospects of rising to any fame were remote so that he was not entirely convinced that the warning would affect him. He also regretted that he could not accept his host's urgent invitation to stay longer in his house when all the other guests had gone, repeating his gratitude for the hospitality given to him the previous unfortunate night.

As foretold by *The Radiant Boy* the Captain rose to very great heights as Viscount Castlereagh. He occupied a prominent political position in Irish affairs, resulting in the Act of Union between England and Ireland in 1801. He was Secretary of War two years later and again in 1807, and was Foreign Secretary from 1812 onwards. With great men like Pitt, Fox, Nelson and Wellington, he steered England through some of its most tragic history. In spite of these great achievements he was very unpopular, even hated by the public.

In 1821 his father died and he became 2nd Marquis of Londonderry. He had reached the climax of fame predicted by *The Radiant Boy*. One year later came the final prophecy of a violent death. He had for some time been in a serious mental condition, which gravely concerned Wellington, who advised that he should be confined to his home in North Cray Place near Dartford in Kent. In spite of the doctor's orders that his razors should be taken away, the Marquis committed suicide by cutting his throat with a penknife. In a bitter, cruel couplet Byron wrote:

He's cut his throat. He? Who?
Why, he who cut his country's long ago.

So far as the author has been able to trace, there has been only one appearance of *The Radiant Boy* in England. This was in Corby Castle in 1803 and is fully detailed in his *Britain's Haunted Heritage*. The two stories are quite incredibly similar, though in the latter case the prophecy was fortunately never carried out, nor did his apparition return.

8   Scotland

Grampian Region: Fyvie Castle: The Ghostly Trumpeter

There could surely be no further encouragement to read about a heavily haunted castle than the opening of an article once published in *The Times* on Fyvie Castle, in the Grampians: 'Like the Castle of Glamis it has its secret chamber; like the Palace of Holyrood it has a "Murder Room" with the ineffaceable blood-stains on the floor. It has its spirit that haunts the great vaulted staircase, bringing warnings of death and disaster like the Irish banshee; and signs and portents to be sought and found in the very stones of the ancient battlements.'

This splendid castle, described as 'the crowning glory of Scottish baronial architecture', with its battlements and fine towers, capped by what might be stone witches' hats, was built in the fifteenth century on the site of an earlier one. It stands on the banks of the River Yunan, close to the village of Fyvie, reached on the B9005. Its finest tower is the Preston Tower, built by Henry de Preston, who was granted all the lands as a reward for capturing the English knight Sir Ralph Percy at the battle of Otterburn. Two other great towers are the Meldrum Tower and the Gordon Tower, named for families who were descendants of Henry de Preston, the owner in 1905 being created Baron Leith of Fyvie. The many hauntings are all related to these families.

One of the weather-worn statues ornamenting the roof is of a figure blowing a trumpet, whose ghost still haunts the castle and who has become known as 'the Trumpeter of Fyvie', its notes bringing warning of death or disaster to the owner of the castle.

Andrew Lammie was deeply in love with Agnes Smith, the daughter of a local miller. The parents strongly objected to this and begged the laird of the castle, then one of the Gordons, to banish him, which he did, sending him to Edinburgh. There he died, but he began haunting the castle.

Another version of the legend was far more sinister and frightening. Andrew was in love with the daughter of the steward of the castle, whose laird also fancied her, desiring her as his mistress. To turn his desire into reality, he ordered a press-gang to abduct Andrew and put him aboard a ship going on long voyages. Then he was captured by pirates and sold as a slave. Years later he managed to escape and return to the castle, only to find the girl he loved was dead, his own death following shortly after. His spirit returned to the castle, for he had vowed when alive to have his revenge on the laird. As the trumpeter he was in life, he haunts the castle regularly, always presaging death to the owner by his trumpeting loudly and continuously as he strides round and in the castle.

The mysterious Green Lady is another ghost, also presaging death every time she appears, and again in revenge for wrongdoing by one of the castle's family. In 1596 Alexander Seton bought the castle and went to live there with his wife, Lilies Drummond, whom he longed and expected to bear him a son to carry on his name, but she produced only a daughter. Lilies had a sister, Catherine, who had a very pretty daughter named Grizel, and the two often came over from Leslie Castle, not far away, to visit Lilies, who quite unaccountably died in Fife in May 1601. In October the laird of Fyvie married Grizel.

When he took his young bride to the castle, much work was in progress on one of the towers and the great staircase, and the couple were unable to spend their wedding night in the master bedroom, being forced to retire to another room in an older part of the castle, which had to be prepared at once. It was not long before they were awakened by the sound of deep sighing, which they thought must be the wind, waking them intermittently through the night. In the morning, as they moved across the room to the window, they saw with astonishment two words about three inches long deeply incised on the glass upside down, which they soon read as LILIES DRUM-MOND. These words have remained ever since on the pane of glass and were at once accepted by the locals as supernatural, as the room was high up in the castle and it was impossible for anyone to scale the wall in the pitch dark and not make any noise, even when using some tool to scratch the glass.

Over the years gossip, rumours and actual facts have emerged and been recorded. Why was Lilies' death sudden and unexplained? Who had incised her name on the glass and why? Had she been murdered in the castle and her body taken to Fife? Had the laird murdered her to make his hasty marriage five months later to Grizel? Stories were then told of a secret chamber in the castle which no owner would ever dare open, keeping it locked and sealed behind a panelled wall. It began to be known as 'the Murder Room'.

Then the Green Lady made her appearance and added to the mystery. Who was she, and why was she always seen in a long green brocade dress, gliding along the passages, always emerging from the Murder Room at the head of the great staircase and returning to it, disappearing through the closed door? She always had pearls in her ears and a lighted candle in her hand, sometimes seeming as if shimmering in a phosphorescent cloud. Was her murderer her husband, out of revenge for her inability to give him a son and heir to carry on his name and possession of the castle? More strangely still, why was her name cut upside down in the glass pane? The mystery has never been solved but rumours and speculations continue, becoming a legend and a tradition.

As if this were not enough in one castle, there is yet another unsolved mystery. This was the doom or curse of the Weeping Stones put upon Fyvie Castle by Thomas the Rhymer. He was the most notable of Scottish wizards, prophets and prognosticators, with the gift of second sight, and was feared by all who came into contact with him as being supernatural. On a terrible night of storm and howling wind this dreaded man appeared at the gates of Fyvie Castle, passing through them and halting at the front door, where he demanded lodging for the night. If the laird at that time had doubted who he was, he soon realized, for Thomas stood in a calm, perfectly dry circle whilst the rain was lashing down and round the castle. When the terrified laird refused him admission, Thomas, still standing on his dry spot, uttered his terrible curse, 'the doom of Sacrilege'.

When, in 1388, Henry de Preston had begun to build his great tower, he had rashly demolished a neighbouring monastery to obtain sufficient stones for it. During the transport three large stones had fallen into the Yunan river. Thomas prophesied that until these three stones were recovered no direct heir would succeed to the title and castle of Fyvie. The curse had begun with Henry de Preston, who had no son but only a daughter who married a Meldrum. There are varying versions of the fate of the stones. One says that two of them were recovered and put into the tower, the third still lost. Another says that the third was recovered and built into a separate chamber of the castle known as 'the lady's bower'. However it was, the castle became known as 'the Castle of the Weeping Stones'. Even so, there are varying versions for the title. One says the one stone is weeping because it is not with the other two. The other, and perhaps more exact definition, says that all the stones weep subject to moisture, however warm and dry the weather. The weeping has always been considered a death warning to the owner of the castle.

In 1928 A.W.M. Stirling published his book *Fyvie Castle*, in which he states the following facts: 'Only one stone can be located, that which presumably was in "my lady's bower" and which now reposes – a curious link with the far-away days of Thomas the Rhymer – in the charter-room at Fyvie, where at times it is bone-dry, and at others exudes sufficient moisture to fill the two wooden bowls in which it rests.'

Lothian: Roslin Castle: The Phantom Flames

The village of Roslin is on the A6094 road about eight miles south of Edinburgh. Near it are the fourteenth-century ruined castle and Roslin Chapel, visited by thousands of visitors each year to see its supremely beautiful interior of incomparable medieval Gothic architecture. The chapel was founded in 1446 by William St Clair, Prince of Orkney, the chancel only being built and the transept begun. The St Clairs died out in 1778, when the estates passed to the Erskines, earls of Rosslyn.

The legend of the phantom flames of Roslin Chapel is one of the most extraordinary, if not unique, stories in the history of supernatural manifestations. Its 'wondrous blaze' was a warning of death to the head of the family. Towards the end of the seventeenth century the chapel was desecrated by a mob and might easily have been as much a ruin as the castle, had not General St Clair first repaired it and his descendants continued the work of preservation which finally produced the architectural marvel the 'Apprentice Pillar', a gem of stone carving unequalled in the world, supporting its beautifully sculpted arch.

The story of its origin is that the mason chosen to carry out the work found himself unable to continue without deeper study of his art and absented himself for a long period to help him produce a masterpiece. In the meantime the apprentice left to carry on with general work decided to try his hand with the pillar. It became an increasing wonder of stone until, now working feverishly and inspired by what he had achieved, he finished the pillar just before the mason returned, who, seeing the pillar in all its perfection, seized a hammer and, in an outburst of terrifying jealous anger, struck the apprentice on his head, killing him. The face of the apprentice was later carved by another mason beneath a frieze of stone leaves in the south-west corner of the chapel.

Strangely enough it is not the ghost of this young apprentice who haunts the chapel, though after his murder local people believed that it did, just as they believed the older legend of a supernatural female figure who guards a vast treasure under the foundation ruins of the castle, who would not leave her post until the blast of a trumpet should release her and the treasure return to the St Clairs. Beneath the chapel floor are the vaults containing the bodies of the St Clair barons, who were always buried in full armour and not 'useless coffins', a fact disclosed in a seventeenth-century manuscript of one of the family, quoted by Sir Walter Scott:

> When my good father was buried, his corpse [a long deceased Baron of Roslin] seemed to be entire at the opening of the cave; but when they came to touch his body, it fell into dust. He was laying in his armour, with a red velvet cap on his head, on a flat stone; nothing was spoiled, except a piece of the white furring that went round the cap, and answered to the hinder part of the head. All his predecessors were buried after the same manner, in their armour; late Rosline, my good father, was the first that was buried in a coffin, against the sentiments of King James the Seventh, who was then in Scotland, and several other persons well versed in antiquity, to whom my mother would not hearken, thinking it beggarly to be buried after that manner.

The haunting of Roslin Chapel by the supernatural manifestation of flames has been immortalized by Sir Walter Scott in his 'Lay of the Last Minstrel':

> O'er Roslin all that dreary night
>   A wondrous blaze was seen to gleam;
> 'Twas broader than the watch-fire light,
>   And redder than the bright moonbeam.
>
> It glared on Roslin's castled rock,
>   It ruddied all the copse-wood glen;
> 'Twas seen from Dryden's groves of oak,
>   And glimpsed from cavern'd Hawthornden.

Seemed all on fire that chapel proud,
  Where Roslin's chiefs uncoffin'd lie;
Each baron, for a sable shroud,
  Sheathed in his iron panoply.

Seemed all on fire, within, around,
  Deep sacristy and altars pale;
Shone every pillar, foliage-bound,
  And glimmered all the dead men's mail.

Blazed battlement and pinnet high,
  Blazed ev'ry rose-carved buttress fair.
So still they blaze when fate is nigh
  The lordly line of Hugh St Clair.

Strathclyde Region: Inveraray Castle: The Battle in the Sky

The great Scottish castle of Inveraray, for over two centuries the home of the dukes of Argyll, attracts many thousands of tourists from all over the world each year. It is built of blue-grey chlorite slate and stands proudly on the edge of Loch Fyne, its four flanking towers giving it an almost medieval look. It is surrounded by immense parklands and trees and has its own supernatural world consisting of the phantom harper, the hovering ravens and the phantom galley, the last two always appearing when one of the Campbell chiefs is dying. The galley is blazoned in the second and third quarters of the Campbell coat of arms.

The ghostly galley appears to have three people on board, one of whom is supposed to be a saint connected with St Columba. It has been seen by many people as it passes silently up the loch to land at a particular point, pass overland, then vanish at St Columba's holy place, given to the Church by the early Campbells. The galley is said to have been seen only by a Campbell or a Highlander, though others have reported seeing it.

Lord Halifax, in his *Ghost Book*, relates his experience of the phantom harper. Just before the outbreak of World War I he was staying with the new Duke, Niall Campbell (whose uncle had died in May 1914), together with Lady Elspeth, Niall's sister. They were having tea in the Green Library when suddenly Lord Halifax was startled by a tremendous noise like a pile of heavy books falling at his side. No one said a word but he noticed a swift exchange of glances between the Duke and his sister. After tea the Duke told him that both he and his sister had seen his reaction, but his sister would explain later.

The next day Halifax and Lady Elspeth were walking in the gardens when she told him that the noise he had heard was caused by the harper, hanged in the seventeenth century by Montrose's men, who had moved up the glen to catch the Marquess of Argyll. She told him that he always appeared in the Campbell tartan, that he was gentle and harmless and only paid attention to 'the elect', so that Lord Halifax must consider himself one of those.

The harper was known affectionately in the castle as 'the little man'; other guests had seen him, and one who had taken her own harp into her room was wakened in the night by someone playing it, though no one was visible. Lady Elspeth later wrote to Lord Halifax telling him 'the little harper' had been very active about the time of the funeral of the late Duke.

Later, again a guest at the castle, Lord Halifax was taken seriously ill, being placed in 'the Archie Room' above the Green Library. During this time he was constantly aware of a presence, especially when he used the turret as a sitting-room. He said nothing until he was leaving, when, in answer to his question as to why he had been put in that particular turret, Lady Elspeth replied: 'For your own good. My aunt Lady Mary Glyn, who was so ill lately, would have died if she had not been placed in that room.'

Even more remarkable than these phantoms was the battle in the sky which took place in broad daylight on 10

July 1758, when three people witnessed this most extraordinary phenomenon. They were the distinguished physician Sir William Hart, a friend of his and a servant, who were all walking together in the castle grounds. One of them looked up to the sky and gave a cry of amazement as he pointed upwards. There they unbelievingly watched great numbers of soldiers in the uniform of the Highlanders attacking a fort defended by what seemed to be a French garrison. The three were speechless, for, as if they were watching such an action on television today, all the details of a battle were taking place before their eyes. The Highlanders were forming a human ladder up the walls of the fort, so that others could climb up, only to be thrown down by the garrison soldiers, the smoke from their muskets floating across the battlefield covered with dead bodies. Then, in a flash, the whole scene vanished.

Two ladies, the Misses Campbell, arrived shortly afterwards at the castle in great excitement, for they, also, had seen the phantom battle, describing it in very clear detail and with great enthusiasm for what they considered to be a mirage or a miracle, thus corroborating everything the other three had seen.

Two years before the phantom in the sky appeared, war between Britain and France had broken out; it was to become known in history as 'the Seven Years War'. All five witnesses knew for certain that the Highlanders were abroad, fighting, for Britain was at war with France at that time. They knew also that Duncan Campbell, Master of Inverawe House, which was some miles north of Inveraray Castle, was in the army and serving abroad, but were unsure where. There could only be speculation, therefore, as to where the battle they had seen was taking place, nor had they the slightest idea as to the number of Highlanders engaged in it. What they did know was that it was in America, for word had reached Scotland some time previously that part of the British army was stationed at a place called Albany, preparing to do battle with the French over disputed territory in the American colonies.

It was many weeks later that an official bulletin announced in Scotland that a great battle had taken place against the French, when a concentrated attack on the enemy had been made at a fort called Ticonderoga on Lake George. There had been heavy casualties among the Highlanders: 300 men killed and as many wounded. Then came the most startling statement of all, announcing the date of the battle, which was 10 July 1758, the exact date of the battle in the sky the five witnesses had seen many weeks before. Such an example of the supernatural world can surely be a challenge to those who do not believe in that world.

9 Wales

Dyfed: Milford Haven: Very Remarkable Phantoms

The ghosts of Wales are countless, seemingly everywhere and with every variety of the supernatural, so that it is never surprising to discover one in any part of that beautiful country. A phantom funeral is not uncommon, a haunted ship is rare, but a phantom ship is rarer still, yet they are all to be found in Dyfed. All of them are fully documented by the people concerned in the three dramas.

The first account, a spectral funeral, was given in *Notes and Queries* in July 1858, when the writer recorded a phantom funeral witnessed by seven or eight members of the same family, who were gathered together one fine summer evening in Milford Haven, between the hours of eight and nine o'clock, talking and gazing across the brook and a couple of meadows separating them from the parish church. Suddenly they saw with astonishment a funeral procession slowly winding its way towards the church. They watched the coffin borne on the shoulders of the mourners. The distance was too great for the family to recognize the men but, as the cortège drew near to the church porch, they distinctly saw the face of their friend the clergyman coming to meet it. They saw him precede the mourners into the church and after a while come out and move towards a part of the churchyard where the final rites were to be carried out.

So amazed were they at what they saw, for no funeral was ever held at that time of the day and they knew of no one who had died, that a messenger was sent to find out what was happening. They were even more amazed when the messenger returned to say that the church was locked, there had been no one there at all, and that on enquiring he was told there had not been a funeral for several days. Even more remarkable was the fact that a few days later a neighbour of the family died and was buried in the precise spot in the churchyard towards which the phantom funeral had moved.

The writer of this story, a Mr John Pavin Phillips, admitted that one member of his family was gifted with second sight, but certainly no others assembled that night. He did, however, record his mother's seeing what proved to be a phantom ship in that same year. He writes:

> My mother lived in a house on the banks of one of the many creeks or *pills* with which the beautiful harbour of Milford Haven is indented. In front of the house is a large court built on a quay wall to protect it from the rising tide. The tide was out so the creek was empty. In this court my mother was walking one fine evening enjoying the moonlight and the balmy summer breeze. Suddenly my mother's attention was aroused by hearing the sound of a boat coming up the pill, the measured dip of the oars in the water and the noise of the revolution in the rowlocks were distinctly audible. Presently she heard the keel of the boat grate on the gravelly beach by the side of the quay wall. Greatly alarmed as nothing was visible she ran into the house and related what she had heard. A few days afterwards the mate of an East Indiaman which had put into Milford Haven for the purpose of undergoing repairs, died on board, and his coffined corpse was brought up the pill and landed on the very spot where my mother heard the phantom touch the ground.

The story of the haunted HMS *Asp* might never have been disclosed had Captain Aldridge, who had been appointed to it, not kept a faithful account of all his experiences and finally revealed them to the *Pembrokeshire County Guardian* on 15 March 1867.

HMS *Asp* was a survey vessel based in Pembroke Dock. In 1850 Captain Aldridge reported to the dockyard to assume command of the ship, whose reputation, he was told by the superintendent, was not all that good, because there had been several accounts of haunting. Though not a sceptical man, Captain Aldridge, like most sailors, had superstitions about the behaviour of the sea, which he had learned never to trust, though always to respect, and he was prepared to take on the challenge.

'It's not the sea that is going to give you trouble more than it can do, it's the crew. You won't get anyone to sail on her round here, they just won't apply.'

In spite of this friendly warning, Captain Aldridge decided to take on the job and at once began to organize shipwrights to carry out the many duties before he could sail. As he found no difficulty in getting the men, he was taken aback when at the end of the week they took their pay but refused to sign on as a crew. Indeed, they even implored him not to sail in her as she was an unlucky ship because of her ghosts and queer happenings, all of which confirmed what the superintendent had first warned him about. After some while, however, Aldridge managed to persuade sufficient crew to man the ship as far as the Dee estuary in North Wales, where he took on an officer, a steward, a cook and a crew before setting sail.

It was not long before he had his first experience of ghosts. It was his custom after the evening meal to sit in his cabin quietly reading, or preferably with an officer who would read aloud to him. His cabin was separated from another by a companionway ladder. No one could leave or board the ship without the Captain's seeing him. Suddenly, one night, while the officer was reading, Captain Aldridge heard loud noises from the aft-cabin next to his, on the other side of the companionway, which was always kept empty but unlocked. The officer put down his book, went quickly next door, banged violently on the door and told whoever was inside to make less noise. On returning to the other cabin, he had just resumed reading when even more noise emanated from the aft-cabin. This time he took a lighted candle and, pushing the door back, began reprimanding whoever it was, only to find no one there. 'He rushed back quicker than he went,' the Captain recorded, but admitted that his fear was equal to the officer's. He decided to make a personal investigation, but all was silent in the empty cabin and nothing seemed to be disturbed on the bunk or floor. But the noises continued, louder than before.

One night he distinctly heard something or someone move from the aft-cabin into his own. He at once rushed out but there was nothing to be seen or even heard. The next night he heard the same noises as he came aboard but again there was nothing to see. He became very much aware now that the ship really was haunted, especially when the next night the quartermaster burst into his cabin, white-faced and shaking, saying there was a woman standing on the paddle-box, her hands pointing up to the sky. The two immediately rushed out, '...only to find the look-out man in convulsions'. Captain Aldridge himself took the look-out's place for the rest of the night but saw nothing. Nevertheless, he admitted in his record that he lost a great many men each trip: some gave notice which he refused to accept, so they deserted; others would not sign on, as rumours of the haunted ship spread through the docks, telling of a transparent woman appearing with her arms outstretched and pointing to the heavens, striking fear into all who saw the ghost.

Other things were happening to Captain Aldridge, quite apart from the rest of the ship. He would find his bedclothes thrown all over his cabin, or they were snatched from his bunk as he was sleeping. Then there was the ice-cold hand that used to press hard down on his forehead and awaken him, the hand seeming to be severed from its unseen arm. Drawers were opened and slammed shut all by themselves. But it was the constant apparition of the woman that disturbed him most of all, and it is almost impossible to believe how he could continue to sail as he did, yet he endured it for seven long years before being compelled to go into dock for repairs to the ship. He was ordered to berth in Pembroke Dock, where sentries were posted to guard the ship.

It was the sentry posted nearest the ship who had a shock, for his astonished eyes suddenly saw the apparition of a female figure standing on the paddle-box, her arms outstretched, the fingers pointing to the sky, before stepping down to shore and proceeding to walk along the footpath towards him. Lifting his charged musket, he challenged the figure, but she walked straight *through* him. The sentry, petrified at what he had seen, dropped his musket and ran straight to the guardroom. He was intercepted by another sentry, who fired his own musket at the white figure gliding towards him and straight through him. There was consternation in the dockyard, and the sentries refused to mount guard unless it were doubled. But the ghost was never seen again, either in the dockyard or on the ship.

The source of the story about the ghost haunting his ship was never revealed by Captain Aldridge in his account of his experiences, but it is small wonder that the ghost struck such terror into anyone who sailed on HMS *Asp*.

It would appear that the ship had started as a mail packet in Ireland, running between Doneghadee and Port Patrick. It was on one of these trips, when she had docked to unload cargo and passengers, that a stewardess went to check for losses by passengers in their cabins. Upon entering one of the cabins, she saw with horror a beautiful young girl lying on a sleeping-berth with her throat cut from ear to ear. She rushed back on shore to inform the authorities. The ship was at once impounded, sentries were mounted and a full investigation was begun. No reason was ever discovered for such a brutal murder, in spite of years of searching. The ship was finally allowed to sail to Pembroke Dock where Captain Aldridge first took command of her. It was no wonder he had difficulty in signing on crews and might not himself have sailed in her had he known the real and gruesome reason for its being haunted.

Mid Glamorgan: *Dunraven Castle*

The Wrecker

There can be no sharper contrast of ghosts than those haunting Dunraven Castle. One is as horrific as the other is gentle and happy.

Three great families in turn occupied the castle, the Botelers, the Vaughans and the Wyndhams. All the authorities differ widely as to the identity of the ruthless and pitiless wrecker who has become a legend in Welsh folklore.

In the seventeenth century the whole of the British seaboard was open to wreckers of ships, attracting them by false lights to become wrecked on unseen and uncharted rocks where they could be looted and any survivor killed, the corpses robbed of any valuables. Such was the law in those times that any wrecked vessel was automatically the property of the lord of the manor and was known as 'the King's Grace'. As the method of wrecking was not stated and the lords of the manors were totally indifferent to the methods, providing they had their considerable share of the booty, the wreckers also found an easy way of becoming rich. The coast around Dunraven Castle, near Porthcawl, particularly the beach leading to the dangerous rocks known as Witch Point, was wide open to any wreckers, and one, either a Vaughan or a Wyndham, was particularly cruel and fiendish, for he would employ oxen with lanterns tied to their horns, the false lights swaying from side to side as the beasts moved, luring ships to disaster.

There is no evidence that Thomas Wyndham was the wrecker other than in *Transactions of Port Talbot Historical Society*, and although one of the Vaughans was also considered to have been the culprit, the documents of the other two recorders do not seem to offer convincing evidence that the Vaughans, a highly respected local family, reasonably affluent, would have resorted to such evil practices.

There was, in fact, a notorious wrecker in the vicinity known as 'Mat of the Iron Hand' who could well have worked with a Wyndham who became lord of Dunraven when the Vaughans sold the property, and it is probably his ghost that haunts not only the ruined castle but the surrounding area, especially on nights when storms are wild and frightening. Or is it a Wyndham? So dangerous and treacherous can this stretch of the coast be that two of the Vaughan family lost their lives swimming on a summer's day by the rocks known as 'the Swinkers'. Their little boat had broken its moorings and they were trapped by the incoming tide, watched by a number of people unable to help.

Though no one would go out at night, the local people were concerned that Wyndham and 'Mat of the Iron Hand' frequently met; they were also concerned that, since the Vaughans had left the district, there had been one or two wrecks, but no one dared say what he thought. Mat was a particularly vicious and embittered man since the time when, as a pirate, his boat had been captured by order of one of the Vaughans. In a fierce battle Mat had been severely wounded and his hand severed from his arm, so that he had an iron hook. He was tried in the court where Vaughan was a magistrate and deprived of his boat, since when he had sworn a secret oath that he would have his revenge on any occupant of Dunraven Castle. It was then that he turned to the far more lucrative business of wrecking.

There came a night when a fierce storm broke out that could only be a portent of tragedy to any ship at sea, particularly along the part of the coast below Dunraven Castle, where those who dared to look could already see the false lights they knew only too well meant disaster for a ship. Those who had ventured to go out in such a storm had already heard the grinding of a ship as it was smashed to pieces on the rocks, the shouting voices and the waving lanterns of the wreckers, and they knew it was better to be indoors. Most of those on board had no chance of escape from drowning; those few who managed to swim ashore fell exhausted and sodden on the beach to incur a worse fate. It was then that Mat and Wyndham moved in, killing first, then looting and plundering the bodies, using those same lights that had lured them to their death. Wyndham was working quickly, anxious to escape back to the castle to avoid questions and suspicion, when, turning over a body, he found he was bending over the corpse of his only son, who was returning from abroad, where he had been a student for a few years. Now he saw only the white face, the blood of the wound he had given and the family ring he had cut from one of the fingers.

From that moment he lost his reason. On every night marking the anniversary of his crime, his ghost can be both seen and heard, waving its arms with horror, screaming and howling, hurrying along the beach, round the now-ruined castle. Even on a night of storm his screams and cries can be heard.

The Blue Lady

The Blue Lady of Dunraven Castle is altogether a much more gentle figure.

During World War I the fourth Earl of Dunraven permitted Dunraven Castle to become a convalescent home for the wounded. The accounts that followed of the spectre of the Blue Lady were intriguing. It was understood that stories of a ghost from shell-shocked soldiers, whose nerves were shattered, might easily have been hallucinations, requiring only sympathy and understanding before trying to convince them that they had not really seen a ghost. It was a completely different matter when the nurses were consulted, for they were in no doubt at all about the presence of a spirit in the castle, in different rooms where they slept, on and off duty, often in pairs.

The housekeeper at Dunraven also, who had been in the service of the family for many years, gave this account, surely an indication of her truth and sincerity:

> I only saw the apparition once, and that was in the conservatory dressing-room about 12 o'clock at night. I had felt its presence dozens of times, but never saw it till then, when it appeared at the foot of my bed. She (for it was a woman) wore a loose flowing gown more like a dressing-gown of a pale blue colour, hair grey and hanging loosely to her shoulders. She appeared quite calm and in no way troubled, and was quite pleasant to look at. I always wish I had spoken to her to see what would have happened, but I never saw her again. I may say that I never felt her presence except when some member of the family was at the Castle. Lady Emily (*sister of the 4th Earl*) was in the next room the night I saw her, and as I had not been to sleep I am certain I could not have dreamt about it. After seeing it, I felt quite relieved and happy, and never felt nervous afterwards at Dunraven, being sure that it is a lovely spirit and nothing to be afraid of.

Other stories of the Blue Lady came from the nursing sisters, many of whom had seen her. One of them, Sister Mary, gave this account of her experiences:

I went to Dunraven Castle in April, 1917. The bedroom I occupied was known as the Amber Room, overlooking the drive on the second floor. It was about the end of May when I first saw the apparition. I had been in bed some time (I usually retired about 11p.m.), and had been asleep, when I woke suddenly, feeling a draught and rustling in the room. My window was always open to its utmost, and thinking I should have to close it a little, I sat up in bed. The draught ceased, and a figure moved across the room from the door to the fireplace. I waited for a moment, too frightened to move. I then switched on the light, only to find the room empty, but for the moment there was a breeze through the room as though a door had been opened and closed. During this time there was a scent distinctly noticeable which I can only associate with mimosa. The figure had the appearance of that of a woman, small in stature and dressed in a loose, light-coloured garment. It is impossible to give any definite description of the apparition, as the light was only faint. The time of the year was late spring, the hour 11.40 p.m., and the windows were about 4½ feet or more above the floor.

My second experience was on August 14th or 15th. I had not been to sleep, but had just finished reading. My book was not a ghost story. It was Chesterton's 'Victorian Age in Literature', and having concluded the last essay in the volume I put off my light and sat up for a while in bed. It was on this occasion a very bright night, and suddenly the scent of mimosa filled the room. Then I saw my little lady, sitting in a chair which was always near the fireplace, holding out her hands as if to warm them at the fire. Her dress was again light in colour and lacey in appearance. This time I did not switch on the light, but, jumping out of bed, I ran into the next room and stayed the remainder of the night with my neighbour, Sister H. I am not naturally nervous, and being a woman of even temperament I soon forgot the incident.

Nothing further happened till about February or early March. It was at that time that a Canadian Sister came on the staff. She shared my room, and about the second week of her stay we had been in bed some while and I had been asleep, when Sister called to me loudly: 'For God's sake, switch on the light!' I did not do so at once, as I knew quite well what was wrong, having noticed the usual aroma, but I demanded to know what was the matter. She answered: 'Oh, *do* switch the light on quickly.' I obeyed the request, to find Sister G. white with fright. She described how a little figure had come in at the door and stayed for a moment at the foot of her bed and then went over to the fireplace, which was near mine. We talked for over an hour, and then I put out the light. I sat up in bed, trying to reason it all out, and after about a quarter of an hour thinking, I had almost convinced myself of the absurdity of the whole thing, when there in the darkness the figure stood before me. Dimly I saw her for a moment, and then she vanished. That was my last meeting with the Blue Lady. I remained four months longer at Dunraven and in the same room, but never saw her again.

South Glamorgan: St Donat's Castle: The Terrifying Ghosts

It is almost impossible to believe that any castle could be so constantly and unremittingly haunted as this Welsh castle, almost the equal of a Scottish castle, Glamis. It is not recorded if all the successive owners were subjected to such torture; the American tycoon millionaire newspaper magnate William Randolph Hearst being one of the owners. The present owners are the United World College of the Atlantic; there have been very few reported hauntings by thousands of students from all over the world attending courses there.

The unwelcome spectral visitors to the magnificent original Norman castle were many and varied, but the principal one was the ghost of the murdered Lady Stradling, in a trailing silken gown, with high-heeled shoes noisily clicking as she wanders ceaselessly through her castle. The castle was first granted to the ancient and knightly family of eastern people called Easterlings or Oosterlings (later becoming Stradling) who dwelt near the Baltic Sea: in 1090, Sir William de Esterling was awarded it by FitzHamon for his part in fighting for, and afterwards against, the king of Glamorgan. The Stradlings held their castle for seven centuries, the baronetcy becoming extinct in 1738.

Lady Stradling's ghost, known as the proverbial 'White Lady', constantly haunted the Long Gallery, where it is possible she was murdered. She was always accompanied by a pack of howling hounds, regarded as a warning of death in the family. The other ghosts are an inexplicable panther padding its way along the passages and corridors; a mysterious and sinister appearance in one of the bedrooms of a moving light 'having the semblance of a large glaring eye'; an evil-looking old hag like a witch, haunting the armoury; and a phantom pianist playing chords on a piano through the closed and locked lid.

One of the Stradlings was captured by pirates when taking his ship from Wales to Somerset. The notorious Breton pirate named Colin Dolphin released his prisoner on payment of a huge ransom, forcing him to sell several of his manors. His captor was later lured by wreckers' false lights to bring his ship into supposed safety on a stormy night, where it was smashed on the rocks. Colin Dolphin was captured and buried up to his neck in the sand to wait for the incoming tide to drown him, after which his body was hung from the Gibbet Tower of the castle in revenge.

It has never been established which Lady Stradling was murdered or by whom, but it has been stated that a Sir Peter, a very cruel man, was the murderer in the seventeenth century. In 1880 a certain Wirt Sykes wrote a book entitled *British Goblins* in which he described the beautiful White Lady as appearing '...when any mishap is about to befall a member of the house of Stradling ... she wears high-heeled shoes and a long trailing gown of the finest silk ...' as she wanders through the castle and its fine grounds leading to the beach and sea, but Sykes did not know which Lady Stradling it is.

Perhaps the strangest 'mishap that befell the family' was

in the eighteenth century, when Sir Thomas Stradling arranged with his friend John Tyrwhitt to go on the Grand Tour then fashionable for aristocrats. They drew up a pact that, should there be an accident causing the death of one of them, the survivor should claim and inherit the lands on which the castle stood. Sir Thomas died at Montpellier, being killed in a duel on 27 April 1738. There were reports that, on John Tyrwhitt's return to Britain to claim the castle, a fierce and prolonged legal battle followed. In actual fact, there was a grave suspicion that Sir Thomas had been killed by his friend, though this was never proved. In any case, Sir Thomas was the last baronet of the Stradling line, the lands being bequeathed to the Tyrwhitt-Drakes of Shardeloes.

Lord Halifax, in his famous *Ghost Book* published in 1936, gives an accurate and well-documented account of what happened in the castle in 1917. He had received a letter from Mr Charles Stirling who, staying in Scotland, had met a well-known faith-healer, whom he called 'Mr X', '...a man of much piety and obvious sincerity. He told me astounding tales of his experience in exorcising haunted houses in various parts of the country. The enclosed is a literal version of what occurred at St Donat's Castle, Glamorganshire .... You may rely on its being an unembroidered and precise account, as I had it from Mr X's own lips.'

At that time the owner of the castle was a retired naval officer who had found the phenomenal behaviour of the many ghosts intolerable not only to his wife, himself and his children but even to the servants, who would no longer stay. He therefore advertised the prospective sale of the castle in *Country Life*. By a remarkable coincidence, he heard at the same time about Mr X, who had extraordinary powers of healing the sick, which he had discovered at the age of fourteen. He had an amazing record of cases of haunted houses he had delivered from evil spirits by exorcism. The owner unhesitatingly invited him to St Donat's to see what he could do there.

In due course he arrived and, after a full consultation with the owner, was informed of all the ghosts that had taken over the castle and made life impossible. Mr X then retired to the bedroom where the huge, glaring eye of light manifested itself nightly. There he prayed and grappled with the Powers of Darkness. He had requested the owner to sit in the hall with the front door wide open while he began his exorcism. Lord Halifax wrote: 'After a while, as though to mark Mr X's triumph over the evil forces of the place, a great gust of wind suddenly blew out from the room where he was praying, swept down the main staircase and all but carried the owner of the Castle into the garden. From that day and hour the ghostly disturbances completely ceased. All was peaceful in the Castle ....'

Nevertheless, even now local people are convinced the Gibbet Tower is still haunted, nor will they pass the castle after dark, because they say that they can hear the moans and baying of the hounds accompanying the White Lady as her high-heeled shoes click along the passages. They have even seen her in the grounds.

10   The Isle of Man

Peel and Rushen: The Two Haunted Castles:

Peel Castle

The picturesque ruins of the massive fourteenth-century stronghold of Peel Castle have far more hauntings than Rushen Castle, and they are very much more terrifying. The ghost of Eleanor, wife of Humphrey, Duke of Gloucester dominates the castle itself. She was imprisoned there in 1441 by Henry VI for using her powers of black magic to cause him a painful and distressing illness. She was held prisoner for fourteen long years and finally died there. Her two accomplices were her paramour, Roger Bolingbroke, and Margery Jourdemain, the notorious witch of Eye, who made a wax model of the King, which, at midnight, the three carried to a crossroad. There they pierced its eyes with daggers, threw it into a fire and muttered their evil incantations to Satan, who would help them to dispose of the King. The King ordered that Bolingbroke be tortured and hanged, Jourdemain burned as a witch in Smithfield, the Duchess end her days in Peel Castle.

For many years the grounds were haunted by an unseen creature which shrieked and howled during the night, keeping the residents awake. One night they decided to go in a party into the grounds and try to discover what or who it was. Just after midnight, according to *Hoods Magazine*, they suddenly heard, quite near, the ghastly, moaning howl, followed by yapping and howling that could only have come from an animal. They stood petrified by the sight of a huge black form leaping and bounding through a stream towards the woods, where it uttered the most diabolical sounds before disappearing, leaving the terrified watchers running back to the castle.

There was, however, an even worse and far more notorious phantom which has become a legend not only in the Isle of Man but throughout the world, named the Mauthe Doog or Moddey Dhoo or Dhog, meaning part devil, part dog. The island historian Waldron states that this phantom animal used to haunt the grounds, so that this might well have been the phantom the residents saw, before it came into the castle itself and finally into the guardroom of the garrison. There, every night, it sat in front of the turf fire the soldiers had made to keep themselves warm on the bitter winter nights. It would arrive regularly at sunset and depart at sunrise, so that the sentries dreaded being on duty during the night. None of them had ever seen it but all had felt its presence, for it never moved away from the turf fire.

A subterranean passage connected the guardroom with the ancient cathedral of St Germain. It was the custom in the mid-seventeenth century, when the most terrible of all Manx hauntings took place (one date gives 1660), for the sentry being relieved, who was in charge of the castle keys, to be escorted by the relief sentry to the captain's apartments, where the relief sentry would be handed the keys by the captain. This was an ancient ceremony carried out nightly. One night the relief sentry had been drinking too much, but, surprisingly, that had gone unnoticed by the captain. When the two were dismissed to return to the guardroom, the relief sentry suddenly boasted that he was going to try to discover what went on that they were all scared of; he was going to do just that.

In spite of advice and protestations from the others, he went off down the passage, which was pitch dark and eerie, his footsteps on the cobbles echoing into the guardroom. After a few minutes terrible screams broke out, petrifying the soldiers in the guardroom, freezing them with stark fear so that no one dared to move to try to see what was happening. Suddenly there was a silence that could be heard; then, slowly, as if dragging along, the sounds of the returning sentry came to their ears, and almost immediately his stumbling figure crashed into the guardroom, onto the floor. He was shaking and trembling, his eyes were wild and frightening, his face as white as chalk. They carried him away, and three days later he died.

Just before his death he was able to tell what had happened to him. He said that on entering the captain's apartment he had seen the Mauthe Doog in the captain's chair.

Those who in the past claimed to see the phantom hound could only describe it as having the form of a huge dog. They said it possessed the power of harming people who were evil and said or did wicked things. Its origin is believed to date back to pagan times when, traditionally, black magic was practised by many people in the Isle of Man. Waldron does not record whether the sentry had seen the last appearance of the dog, and there is no documentary evidence that it was. Only the sentries could have been able to answer that question; surely that would have been recorded?

Rushen Castle

The splendid castle, whose building commenced in 1150, overlooks the quiet and beautiful harbour of Castletown, former capital of the Isle of Man; it was presented to the islanders by King George V in 1929, as an expression of gratitude for the part the Manx people had played in World War I. It is traditionally the island home of the living king or queen of England, who is known as Lord of Man. In the fourteenth century it was the palace of the Norse kings, becoming successively the House of Keys, a prison, a lunatic asylum and a barracks. Not surprisingly it is also haunted.

Deep down underneath the castle were the torture chambers and the prisons, and from quite early in its history this part of the castle was believed to be haunted by giants. The legend is pagan and probably spread from the ninth century when the tall, rapacious Vikings invaded the island in an horrific onslaught on the people. Waldron's account of the giants is a bizarre one, but so implicitly did the islanders believe in these spectres that it passed into the folklore of the island. There was a time when any man daring enough to endeavour to see them was said never to return; therefore the authorities sealed up all the passages and doors leading to the vaults.

There came a day, many years later, when a man was so determined to investigate the authenticity of those rumours that he was permitted to investigate – without any liability whatsoever on the authorities. He took with him a ball of pack-thread to mark his path through the pitch-dark passages and chambers. Already perturbed by the eeriness of the unknown, and just when he began to wonder if he had not been stupid, he saw far ahead a light. Delighted, he moved as fast as he could towards it until his astonished eyes saw a magnificent mansion, candles lighting up every room. He had to knock three times before the door was opened by a servant who demanded to know what he wanted there.

'I would go as far as I can,' answered the adventurer. 'Be so kind as to direct me, for I see no passage but that dark cavern through which I have come.'

The servant told him that he must go straight through the house and out of the back door, then walk a considerable way until he came to another house. He obeyed his instructions, proceeding along what seemed an endless passage until he came to the other house, even more magnificent, with every room blazing with lanterns and all the windows open. Instead of knocking, he stepped up on a little bank and saw a vast chamber in which was a large table. Let Waldron give his own version:

> On the table, extended at full length, lay a man or rather monster, at least fourteen feet long and ten or twelve round the body. This prodigious fabric lay as if sleeping with his head upon a book, with a sword by him, answerable to the hand which he supposed made use of it. The sight was more terrifying to our traveller than all the dark and dreary mansions through which he had passed …. He resolved, therefore, not to attempt an entrance into a place inhabited by persons of such monstrous stature, and made the best of his way back to the other house, when the same servant who reconducted

him informed him that if he had knocked at the second door he would have seen company enough, but could never have returned ...

When he asked the servant the name of the house and its owner, he was told that such things must never be revealed. He was then shown out and made his way back through the long, dark passages, filled with terror at what he had seen, reaching safety and sunlight at last. The historian Waldron, with characteristic drollery, adds: 'Whoever seems to disbelieve it is looked on as a person of weak faith.' It is hoped that he means only the islanders.

11   The Isle of Wight

Knighton Gorges: The Black Knight

Two massive gateposts, a terrace, a walled garden and a gardener's cottage are the eerie and mysterious relics of a once great Norman manor house, known as Knighton Gorges. It is still one of the most haunted places in the island, if not in the United Kingdom, most especially by the dreaded Black Knight, the hoofbeats of his galloping horse having terrified countless people.

The manor house was once an impressive grey stone building with massive walls, a buttressed turret covering a thirty-foot-deep dungeon below, and terraced walled gardens sloping to a willow-covered pool, as impregnable as it was impenetrable. It was there that Eudo de Morville, one of the four knights who murdered Thomas à Becket during the reign of Henry II, found refuge. His grandson-in-law was one of the first three Sir Ralph de Gorges, all Crusaders and probably Knights Templar. The third Sir Ralph's daughter married Sir Theobald Russell of Yelverdon, who, in 1340, was severely wounded in a battle with the French invaders at Nunwell, dying of wounds in his bedroom, known as 'the Room of Tears'. It was named so by Anthony Dillington, who bought the manor in 1565, for the room was haunted by constant sobbing, causing those who heard it also to sob, whereupon the sound would cease in the room.

Another Dillington was knighted, as Sir Robert, by Queen Elizabeth I but was later arrested and imprisoned in the Fleet prison. Yet another Robert was so mean that he removed all the hay from his stable-racks whenever mounted visitors or guests arrived at the manor house. His issue squandered everything they inherited, with riotous abandon.

Each successive member of each family seemed to have caused the many and various phantoms in the manor. Wicked deeds, murder, agonizing wails, coaches and horses in the night, a spectral hound (whining from the bleeding wounds his master had given him, who creeps round the garden) and mysterious sounds of music from a sealed room all seem to combine to exist happily together.

Sir Tristram Dillington, who died in 1712, was the most outstanding of all the family's members. He was MP for Newport, rich, generous, loved by all who knew him, holding high revels at the manor. Tragedy suddenly struck him down. Within a fortnight, his wife and four children, including his heir, died of a mysterious fever and were buried in Newchurch parish churchyard. The shock turned him into an embittered man, morose and lonely, and within weeks he had died in most mysterious circumstances of which a strange legend existed. It is said that his butler, faithful and loyal, had closely watched his master and saw him, on 4 July 1712, commit suicide by throwing himself into the deep pond at the bottom of his garden.

At that time all the possessions of a suicide were confiscated by the Crown. Sir Tristram had two sisters, both spinsters, and in order to save their rightful inheritance the butler destroyed the girth of his master's favourite horse, Thunderbolt, let the horse wander loose round the pond and ran for a servant to help him get Sir Tristram's body out of the pool, telling him the horse had thrown him into the pond. His reward was a small farm at nearby Brading, as a present from the two sisters. Sir Tristram's ghost was often seen by many people, walking sadly and slowly round the gardens and the pool.

Maurice George Bassett was the next to possess Knighton Gorges, in which he ran a Hellfire Club; visitors included Sir Joshua Reynolds, the Garricks, the ugly John Wilkes and Lady Worsley, who had left her husband for Bassett. Sir Richard Worsley sued Bassett for £20,000 but was awarded only a shilling – 'being adjudged privy to his wife's prostitution'. The scandal became sensational in London society, and Lady Worsley was outraged by hawkers selling broadsheets and pamphlets quoting the case and the accusation of the court against her.

Bassett, described by those who knew him as 'an unscrupulous bigot', soon gave further proof of those words. His daughter had fallen in love with a clergyman and told her father she was going to marry him. In an outburst of unreasonable temper, Bassett forbade the marriage, which resulted in the couple eloping and getting married. Bassett at once disinherited his daughter and threatened them never to set foot in Knighton Gorges again. The couple ignored these threats, which they did not believe he would carry out. It was just a question of waiting for him to relent.

In November of that year Bassett ordered in a team of masons and gangs of labourers, workmen and demolition experts, who ruthlessly obeyed his orders not to leave a stone standing of his splendid house. He himself moved into the gardener's cottage, where he died on 21 December. Thus his threats and revenge were fulfilled, and one of the most beautiful ancient houses on the island was obliterated forever, though the hauntings went on as before, so that no one dared to go near what was left.

The phantom of the Black Knight is even now feared by local people, who swear they have heard the thundering hoofbeats of his jet-black horse. They have described him as tall, dressed in a medieval costume, his black cloak streaming behind him as he gallops across fields, lanes and roads. He rides on moonlit nights and always on New Year's Eve. Some say he is headless, and legend says there was a knight living in Knighton Gorges Manor House who was cursed by a wizard that caused his death and his ghost. It might well have been Eudo de Morville who took refuge in the manor house after his criminal deed and was cursed to ride forever on his black horse as a penance.

12   The Channel Islands

Guernsey: The Haunted Wells

It seems certain from considerable research into the history of ghosts that Guernsey and Jersey have the earliest dated ones, which go back as far as the possession of the islands by the Normans. The story of the Haunted Well has a probable date of 1284, as recorded in a manuscript of Bailiffs compiled in 1650, which mentions the name of the evil Gaultier de la Salle, whose ruthless and pitiless persecution of a peasant caused his (Gaultier's) ghost to haunt the well, of whose water he could never gain possession in his lifetime.

The existence of wells goes far back in history to the Old Testament, vital as they were for travelling Bedouin, caravans carrying silks, gold, rich garments, perfumes and dates across the limitless deserts. Every well was vital to the camels which drew the caravans and was charted in the mind only, just as the earliest sea charts were, before they were recorded on maps. The owner of a well had a special right, an hereditary right, passed down through generations from the earliest owner and jealously protected and guarded.

Such a right belonged to an otherwise desperately poor peasant in Guernsey named Massy. His well stood in a small field, little more than a *'verge'* of land (old French for 'brink' or 'border') at the back of Gaultier de la Salle's estate, the Ville au Roi, a splendid fortified manor house, occupied by Gaultier in about 1284 as the privilege of a Bailiff, Lieutenant Governor, chief magistrate and Receiver of the Crown Revenues, to give him his full title. (In the fifteenth century the house was extended into a magnificent mansion, though still preserving much of its original structure, such as a tower, open timber roof, slits

for arrows in the stonework and remains of an arched
gateway surrounded by considerable lands, farm
buildings and enclosures for cattle.)

Thus the well was in Gaultier's possession, but not the
right to draw water from it, which belonged to Massy,
who could forbid the Bailiff or any of his servants to draw
water without his, Massy's permission.

Gaultier's displeasure rapidly grew into hatred for
Massy, whom he regarded as a serf with no rights at all to
the well, since there was no record of such in existence. In
those times peasants had no claims to property at all as far
as those above them were concerned. The Normans
neither gave nor acknowledged the ancient rights of any
of the islanders. Gaultier knew only too well that there
were several ways of disposing of a peasant. He could kill
him himself or have him assassinated by someone else,
but even in those wild days open violence was dangerous
and would arouse suspicions. He also knew very well that
this ancient right to the drawing of water existed in the
islands and could not be taken away from anyone who
had inherited it. Any man who abused this heritage would
automatically be sentenced to death.

Massy lived alone; he had no living relatives. Therefore,
when he died, the well could be put up for sale and
obviously bought by the Bailiff. There was only one way to
obtain the well, and Gaultier was not long in finding a
solution in a brutal and evil way.

One of the most rigorous laws of the islands was the
death penalty for theft of any kind. Thus, if Massy could
be proved to have been a thief, he would automatically
receive the death penalty, and the land pass to the Crown;
since Gaultier held the office of Receiver of the Crown
Revenues, he foresaw no difficulty in obtaining the well
and thus the right of inheritance for his own family. It was
a fiendish calculation even from one renowned in the
island for his ruthlessness and evil ways, for which he was
hated by very many islanders.

On a certain day, therefore, Gaultier sent for one of his
servants and, under the severest threats of death should
he ever disclose the secret to anyone, handed him three
fine silver goblets, instructing him to hide them in a

certain corn-stack he had carefully selected, telling his servant that it was to prevent such precious goblets being stolen. He then cunningly caused suspicion to circulate that Massy had stolen the cups, followed by a direct accusation against the helpless peasant, which led to his arrest and imprisonment to await trial and the inevitable death sentence. This was swiftly hastened by Gaultier, and on the day of the trial, in spite of Massy's most passionate declarations of his innocence, the sentence of death was passed.

The date of execution was also hastened, and on the appointed day the Bailiff proceeded to the court house prior to the execution. Before leaving the Ville au Roi, however, he sent another of his servants to order the farm labourers to take down one of the cornstacks and put it in the barn. The magistrates were already assembled in the court house when, as Gaultier moved across to take his seat, a messenger, almost breathless with the exertion of his running, shouted out his news to the Bailiff.

'The cups are found!'

'Fool!' cried the Bailiff. 'Did I not tell thee *not* to touch *that* rick? I know ...'

In the hushed court the magistrates watched his confusion in silence as he suddenly realized his appalling mistake. Orders to stay the execution were immediately commanded by the Jurats, (magistrates) who retired for the fullest consultation on so grave a matter. The investigation was one of the most searching in the history of the court. The whole fiendish plot came to light, and when the magistrates returned and took their places, the sentence of death on Massy was reversed and passed on Gaultier, to be carried out immediately. All his property was given to the Crown, excluding the well.

On his way to the gibbet, Gaultier paused to receive the Holy Sacrament at a place called 'La Croix au Baillif', 'the Bailiff's Cross', long ago destroyed but still known by that name. The field in the parish of St Andrew's – the customary place for executions – was called 'Les Galères', and was not far from a mill called 'Moulin de l'Echelle', because the miller was obliged to provide the ladder (*l'échelle*) to the gibbet as part of his tenure. In that field the

Bailiff Gaultier de la Salle was hanged before an excited and jubilant crowd, no doubt including Massy himself.

For centuries all those places, including the well, were haunted; no one dared go there by day or night. The very road the Bailiff used to reach the gibbet was known as 'la rue de l'Ombre de la Mort', 'the Shadow of Death road'. Every night at the hour of Gaultier's execution and during the night, a huge headless phantom of a hound has been seen. The place became called 'the Evil Place'. Those peasants brave enough to strike at the phantom dog with their cudgels met no resistance, and all were convinced that it was the unquiet and guilty spirit of the Bailiff returning to the gibbet along the Shadow of Death road.

Spectral black and headless dogs have always been widely seen and heard in all countries. It has been suggested that animals have their own soul but when they die it often passes into human beings, but there has never been an authentic reason given for these apparitions. Often our ancestors buried a warrior's horse and dog with him, so that they might enter another life together, but there is no cogent reason for any dog entering the spirit of the evil Bailiff Gaultier de la Salle.

Even more haunted than the well of the Ville au Roi is the Holy Well of St George in the parish of Castel, otherwise Catel, the largest in Guernsey. So badly was it haunted at one time that no one would dare go there. It stands today in the beautiful estate of St George as a part of the ruins of the once splendid medieval chapel. This once most sacred spot was sanctified by St George himself, who visited the island centuries ago and established the well bearing his name. It is surmounted by a cross and hood under which is a niche to receive coins as alms from those who had been cured. The saint blessed all the buildings and commanded the well to produce water of such purity that all manner of illnesses could be remedied. According to legend, the cures were countless, and those people who drank its waters had more faith in the water than in medicine.

The islanders have always been superstitious about devils, witches, apparitions, demons and ghosts, so that it may not have been so terrible for them to accept the successive hauntings. For a very long time, therefore, the well, the chapel and the adjoining cemetery were venerated, and parents and their children came constantly to the well, placing their silver coins in the niche in gratitude for their healing. It was a custom of the Romans to do such things: in Rome and Bath today people drink the waters and offer coins. Later still, young girls sought other properties they believed the water might possess. It became a custom for those seeking a husband to visit the well to peer down into it and seek in the water the face of a future husband. This could be achieved only by fasting and silence on the part of the girl, who was to visit the well for nine successive mornings, depositing each time a silver coin in the niche 'as an offering to the saint', believing that she would be 'assured of matrimony within nine times nine weeks'.

Then there came a time of terror, for, amid the shrubbery bordering the cemetery and an ivy-covered wall, an apparition of a young girl was seen. She moved noiselessly and very slowly, wringing her hands, distractedly weeping, seeming to pass more time in the cemetery than in any other part of the area. She had been a devoted novitiate of the chapel and was the daughter of elderly parents who had not seen her for some days, nor had she attended her offices and services in the chapel. Enquiries began. A few days later her mangled body was found by the dangerous Hamois Rocks in Rocquaine Bay, so badly smashed as to be almost unidentifiable. It was the body of 'Marie the novitiate', as she was known by all. So disfigured was she that no one suspected murder, and life resumed its normal course, except for the lonely, wandering ghost by the holy well and the cemetery.

There was no logical reason why Marie should have been missing in the first place. She was deeply religious and was a kind and caring girl who was always ready to help anyone in trouble. She was thought by some to be too serious, somewhat melancholy and languid, often crying when suddenly surprised by anyone, generally quiet, self-contained and preferring her own company. On the day of her funeral almost the whole village were mourners. She was naturally buried in the chapel. From that day her ghost began its appearances, wandering round and round the cemetery, but more often staying there for a long period before moving round the whole area. No longer did people go to the holy well, the chapel or cemetery; her ghost became a part of the village, as her real person had been. The years passed, and what had actually happened passed into the legend and folklore of Guernsey.

A very significant burial took place some years later. There had obviously been others since Marie's death, but this time a fresh grave was dug next to the one in which she had been buried. The fresh grave was being finished as the mourners arrived from the service in the chapel, when, before their astonished eyes, some bones fell out from Marie's grave. One of the mourners picked one up and, as he held it in his open palm, he gave a terrible shriek, for blood was flowing from the dried bone. In terror and with shaking hands, he confessed his guilt of the crime he had committed in murdering Marie, whose lover he had been. He was at once seized by two of the men watching what had happened and taken away to the constable, who arrested and imprisoned him to await his trial for self-confessed murder. The subsequent trial was short, sentence of death by hanging being passed.

On the day of his execution he, like the evil Bailiff in the Ville au Roi case, was led to the gibbet in St Andrew's field, after receiving the Holy Sacrament at La Croix au Baillif, named after Gaultier de la Salle in the previous story, thus strangely linking the two hauntings. As suddenly as Marie's ghost had begun its hauntings on the night of her burial years before, it now ceased to haunt the cemetery or chapel or well, for there is no record extant of her re-appearance. The islanders have always called ghosts *'reve-nants'*, 'those who come back'; Marie was no exception in the first place, but after her spirit had been released from its earthbound distress, she had found peace and there was no need to return to her former unhappiness.

Jersey: The Tombelenes: The Place Accursed

Before the year 1462, when the Norman sheepstealers known as 'Moutonniers' invaded Jersey, there was a cave called 'Le Cruex Bouanne' on the rugged north coast of Bouley Bay. Such were the sinister events that took place after that date that the name 'The Place Accursed' was given to it by the islanders. On nights of terrible storms and flashing lightning, haunting cries and screams could be heard above the noise of thunder and heavy seas. These are 'the cries of the Tombelenes', from the cliffs above the bay. Even today the place is sinister, for what happened there five centuries ago has passed into legend and folklore.

On a night in that year of 1462 the first knitting and social event of the winter, known as 'L'Assise de Veille', coincided with a great festive party being held at the farm belonging to a rich farmer, whose lands were near Bouley Bay. He was celebrating the betrothal of his son, Raulin de l'Ecluse, to Jeanne de Jourdain, the daughter of a neighbour and the most charming and beautiful girl on the island. By a fire made of faggots and clumps of seaweed, the old men sat drinking cider from huge mugs, the women knitting and gossiping, the children dancing figures-of-eight as they hummed the tunes.

At the height of the festivities the company all rose to drink a toast to the young betrothed couple, and then the toast every islander loved to drink, 'Down with all the gallows fodder of Normans!' As they clashed glasses and mugs together, there was a loud hammering on the door, followed by the raucous voice of one of the hated Normans, demanding entry. There followed a silence that could be heard in the room as the eyes of all present turned to the door. Once again there were heavy knocks, and as the old farmer opened it, he was sent spinning by a heavily built brute of a man shouting at everyone, demanding to know why he had been kept waiting.

'Kneel! Kneel! All of you, kneel!' he roared at the company, his fists clenched, his face red with anger. 'We are the conquerors,' he shouted. 'You are the conquered, meeting together to plot against us. Kneel!'

It was then that young Raulin stepped forward. 'No one here will kneel to you. Clear out!'

The Norman glared at him. 'As for you, your account will be settled tomorrow,' he shouted and, turning, he stamped out of the room amidst a roar of laughter from all there.

The festivities were over and, in anxiety and no little fear, the guests began to go home, young Raulin accompanying Jeanne to her house. The wind was rising, distant thunder was heard and Jeanne begged her betrothed to shelter the night from the impending storm with her in her grandfather's house. Raulin only laughed, saying he had no fear, but he agreed to take her dog, Fidèle, back with him. 'You may count on him if there is danger,' she said. 'He will guard you.' They were prophetic words indeed.

The storm increased as he began to walk home, the thunder drowning Fidèle's warning bark as the sound of galloping horses came from behind them. As Raulin turned, one of the riders slashed his face with a whip, felling him to the ground, and as the dog leapt at the horse, the rider stabbed him with his dagger. In a few moments the horsemen had tied Raulin's arms and legs together, blindfolded him and slung him over one of the saddles. Ordered by Raulin to go home, the wounded dog set out for Jeanne's house.

Much later that night Raulin was taken by his now drunken captors to their chief, none other than the brutal Norman who had threatened him, as he found when the bandage was snatched from his eyes. He saw that he was in a cave at the end of which was a blazing fire over which a whole sheep was roasting, perhaps even one stolen from Raulin's own farm.

'My lambs!' shouted the chief to his men. 'You see the

guilty one!' The gang moved forward, their daggers drawn. 'Not that way,' shouted the chief. 'This Jersey dog must be hung.' He pointed to one of the gang who had a sinister, cruel face, a red beard and hair. 'You, Dominic, will do the job.' Raulin was then dragged away to the end of the cave to await his execution.

Fidèle, bleeding badly from his wound, went back home, his piteous cries waking Jeanne, who knew at once that there was danger. Dressing hurriedly, she went out to join the dog, which was already getting the scent and direction of the horses. At great speed they reached the cave, where, to her horror, she saw Raulin with his hands and feet bound, standing erect beneath a dangling noose, the other end held by the executioner. At the far end of the cave stood the brutal Moutonnier who had burst into their betrothal party. In a wild dash, followed by Fidèle, she made straight for the chief, who, surprised at the sudden apparition of a beautiful girl, cried out to the men, 'Get her! She's mine!' Two men rushed forward but in a lightning flash Jeanne seized the dagger from one of them and plunged it into his heart. The dog leapt at the other's throat but, weakened by loss of blood, fell with his victim to the floor as Jeanne swiftly cut Raulin free. The two then moved to confront the chief, who stood with his dagger drawn. As the unarmed Raulin tried to come between the two, the chief drove his dagger deep into Raulin's body. In a simultaneous move Jeanne drove her dagger into the chief's throat. Her piercing shriek of horror echoed and re-echoed round the cave before she began her insane dash towards the beach opposite l'Islet.

The Normans stumbled after her but she was too fast for them in her headlong dash to the sea. They lost sight of her when they reached a large rock between themselves and the sea but began scrambling and climbing it, determined to capture her. The storm had returned as dawn was breaking; the surrounding cliffs echoed with the thunder and were brilliantly lit by the flashes of lightning. Even above the storm, Jeanne's piteous cries to Raulin for help and her shrieks of terror could be heard. The sea was pounding the beach with huge waves coming from Verclut. The Normans suddenly saw her, a desperate figure, her hair and cloak streaming behind her in the wind, her arms outstretched towards the sea as if to stem the waves. Then suddenly a huge wave swept in and snatched her from the rocks, dragging her body out on the ebb towards the horizon. There was one last shriek before her body vanished under the waves – a piercing cry called by the islanders 'the cry of the Tombelenes'.

Search parties sought in vain for the missing lovers all that day. It was ten days later when two fishermen, standing on the cliffs, spotted a body floating on the calm sea; at the same time a number of crows flew from what had always been thought of as a grotto. Hurriedly they rushed back to the village to announce their find and then, led by the crows circling round and round, found the body of Raulin, Fidèle, the slain sheepstealers and the chief, whose body had been picked clean by the crows. Raulin and Jeanne were buried in the churchyard, Fidèle in his old master's garden, and the chief with two of his gang, one the executioner, in a hole near the cave. From that day it was known to the whole island as 'the Place Accursed'.

Since that time, at the approach of violent storms, cries and screams have been heard in and around the cave, and few would dare go near, warned by that terrible 'cry of the Tombelenes' from the spirit of Jeanne de Jourdain for her betrothed, Raulin de l'Ecluse. Not long after the tragedy a dying Norman sent for a priest to confess that he was one of the Moutonniers who had witnessed the murders and thus authenticated the terrible legend.

Principal Sources

Automobile Association, *Country Towns and Villages of Britain* (1985)
Aubrey, J., *Miscellanies* (1696)
——————— *Brief Lives* (1949 edition)
Baring-Gould, S., *Cornish Characters and Strange Events* (1935)
Baxter, B., *The Invisible World* (1691)
Braddock, J., *Haunted Houses* (1986)
Briggs, K.M and Tongue, R.L., *Folktales of England*
Brooks J., *Railway Ghosts*
Burne, C., *Shropshire Folklore* (1883)
Collinson, J., *History of Somerset* (1791)
Clutterbuck, *History and Antiquities of Hertfordshire*
Cox, J.S., *Guernsey Folklore*
Coysh, V., *Guernsey* (1983)
Dale, Owen E., *Footfalls on the Boundary of Another World* (1859)
Day, J.W., *A Ghost Hunter's Guide Book* (1956)
Doyle, A.C., *The Edge of the Unknown* (1930)
Fuller, T., *Worthies of England*
Halifax, Viscount, *Lord Halifax's Ghost Book* (1936)
Hall, T.H., *New Light on Old Ghosts* (1965)
Hanning, P., *Dictionary of Ghosts* (1982)
Hardwick, C., *Traditions, Superstitions and Folklore* (1872)
Harland, J. and Wilkinson, T., *Lancashire Legends* (1873)
Harman, H., *Sketches of the Bucks. Countryside* (1934)
Harper, C.G., *Haunted Houses* (1924)
Hasted, E., *History of Kent* (1797)
Henderson, W., *Notes on the Folklore of the Northern Counties of England and the Borders* (1866)
Hillsdon, S., *Jersey Ghosts and Traditions* (1984)
Hole, C., *Traditions and Customs of Cheshire* (1947)
——————— *Haunted England* (1940)
Hutchinson, W., *History and Antiquities of Cumberland* (1794)
Ingram, J., *Haunted Houses and Family Traditions of Great Britain* (1900)
Jarvis, *Accredited Ghost Stories* (1823)
Johnson, W., *Folk Memory* (1908)
L'Amy, J.H., *Jersey Folklore*
Lane-Clarke, L., *Folklore of Guernsey and Sark* (1880)
Lawrence, B., *Somerset Legends*

Lee, Dr F.G., *Glimpses of the Supernatural* (1875)
Legg, R., *A Guide to Dorset Ghosts*
Lempriere, R., *Channel Islands* (1970)
Maple, E., *The Realm of Ghosts* (1964)
Marc, A., *Haunted Castles* (1974)
Nugent, Lord, *Memorials of John Hampden*
O'Donnell, E., *Family Ghosts and Ghostly Phenomenon* (1933)
———— *Ghosts of London* (1932)
———— *Haunted Britain* (3rd impression)
———— *Ghost Short Stories* (1909)
Palmer, K., *The Folklore of Somerset*
Panson, W., *Skipsea Castle*
Poole, K.B., *Ghosts of Wessex* (1976)
Price, H., *Poltergeists over England*
Robinson, W.S., *Guernsey* (1977)
Roy, C., *Ghosts and Legends* (1975)
Russell, E., *Ghosts* (1975)
Scott, Sir Walter, 'Lay of the Last Minstrel'
Sergeant, P.W., *Historic British Ghosts*
Sherman, M.R., *Ghosts of Glamorgan* (1963)
Sitwell, S., *Poltergeists* (1940)
Spencer, M.R., *Annals of South Glamorgan*
Steadman, G., *Ghosts of the Isle of Wight*
Tongue, R.L., *Folklore of Somerset*
Turner, J., *Ghosts of the South West* (1973)
Underwood, P., *A Gazetteer of British Ghosts* (1971)
———— *Into the Occult* (1972)
———— *West Country Hauntings* (1986)
———— *Haunted London* (1973)
———— *Ghosts of Hampshire and the Isle of Wight*
———— *Ghosts of Wales* (1978)
Wolley, P., *Guernsey Legends*

Series covering counties in this book are:
The King's England, Arthur Mee
Highways and Byways, Various authors
The Buildings of England, Nicolaus Pevsner, ed.
Gentleman's Magazine
Notes and Queries

Also:
Society for Psychical Research
Local Historical Societies, field clubs, county Histories, regional journals, magazines and newspapers
Burke's Peerage, Extinct Peerage and *Landed Gentry*
Country Life
La Société Guernesiaise Documents, 1887, 1883
E. MacCulloch, Guernsey Folklore Documents
Folklore of Jersey (Redberry Press, 1987)

Index